Palgrave Macmillan's Critical Studies in Gender, Sexuality, and Culture

Highlighting the work taking place at the crossroads of sociology, sexuality studies, gender studies, cultural studies, and performance studies, this series offers a platform for scholars pushing the boundaries of gender and sexuality studies substantively, theoretically, and stylistically. The authors draw on insights from diverse scholarship and research in popular culture, ethnography, history, cinema, religion, performance, new media studies, and technoscience studies to render visible the complex manner in which gender and sexuality intersect and can, at times, create tensions and fissures between one another. Encouraging breadth in terms of both scope and theme, the series editors seek works that explore the multifaceted domain of gender and sexuality in a manner that challenges the taken-for-granted. On the one hand, the series foregrounds the pleasure, pain, politics, and aesthetics at the nexus of sexual practice and gendered expression. On the other, it explores new sites for the expression of gender and sexuality, the new geographies of intimacy being constituted at both the local and global scales.

Series Editors:

PATRICIA T. CLOUGH is professor of Sociology and Women's Studies at Queens College and The Graduate Center, CUNY. Clough is on the editorial boards of *Women's Studies Quarterly*, *Body and Society*, *Subjectivity*, *Cultural Studies/Critical Methodologies*, *Qualitative Inquiry*, and *Women and Performance*. Clough is the co-editor of *Beyond Biopolitics: Essays in the Governance of Life and Death* (with Craig Willse, 2011); editor of *The Affective Turn: Theorizing the Social* (with Jean Halley, 2007); and the author of *Autoaffection: Unconscious Thought in the Age of Teletechnology* (2000); *The End(s)of Ethnography: From Realism to Social Criticism* (1998); *Feminist Thought: Desire, Power and Academic Discourse* (1994); and *The End(s) of Ethnography: From Realism to Social Criticism* (1992).

R. DANIELLE EGAN is professor and chair of the Gender and Sexuality Studies Program at St. Lawrence University. Egan is the author of *Dancing for Dollars and Paying for Love: The Relationships between Exotic Dancers and their Regulars* (2006) and co-author of *Theorizing the Sexual Child in Modernity* (with Gail Hawkes, 2010), both with Palgrave Macmillan. She is also the co-editor of *Flesh for Fantasy: Producing and Consuming Exotic Dance* (with Katherine Frank and Merri Lisa Johnson, 2006). She is on the editorial board of *Sexuality and Culture*.

Titles:

Magnus Hirschfeld and the Quest for Sexual Freedom: A History of the First International Sexual Freedom Movement
Elena Mancini

Queer Voices: Vocality, the Uncanny, and Popular Music
Freya Jarman-Ivens

On the Literary Nonfiction of Nancy Mairs: A Critical Anthology
Edited by Merri Lisa Johnson and Susannah B. Mintz

Antarctica as Cultural Critique: The Gendered Politics of Scientific Exploration and Climate Change
Elena Glasberg

The Parallel Lives of Women and Cows: Meat Markets
Jean O'Malley Halley

The Aesthetics of Cute in Contemporary Japanese Art
Yoke-Sum Wong (forthcoming)

The Parallel Lives of Women and Cows

Meat Markets

Jean O'Malley Halley

palgrave
macmillan

THE PARALLEL LIVES OF WOMEN AND COWS

Softcover reprint of the hardcover 1st edition 2012 978-0-230-11518-7

First published in 2012 by
PALGRAVE MACMILLAN®
in the United States—a division of St. Martin's Press LLC,
175 Fifth Avenue, New York, NY 10010.

Where this book is distributed in the UK, Europe and the rest of the world, this is by Palgrave Macmillan, a division of Macmillan Publishers Limited, registered in England, company number 785998, of Houndmills, Basingstoke, Hampshire RG21 6XS.

Palgrave Macmillan is the global academic imprint of the above companies and has companies and representatives throughout the world.

Palgrave® and Macmillan® are registered trademarks in the United States, the United Kingdom, Europe and other countries.

ISBN 978-1-349-29651-4 ISBN 978-1-137-07169-9 (eBook)
DOI 10.1057/9781137071699

Library of Congress Cataloging-in-Publication

Halley, Jean O'Malley, 1967–
The parallel lives of women and cows : meat markets / by Jean O'Malley Halley.
p. cm.—(Critical studies in gender, sexuality, and culture)

1. Halley, Jean O'Malley, 1967– 2. Feminist theory. 3. Violence. 4. Women—Violence against. 5. Women—Identity. 6. Meat industry and trade. 7. Animal welfare. I. Title.

HQ1190.H347 2012
305.4201—dc23 2012017942

A catalogue record of the book is available from the British Library.

Design by Newgen Imaging Systems (P) Ltd., Chennai, India.

First edition: November 2012

10 9 8 7 6 5 4 3 2 1

Transferred to Digital Printing in 2013

For Andy and Katie,
and our mother, who found the way out,
and to Isaiah and Kathleen, beat of my heart,
with endless love

Contents

Acknowledgments

Portions of this book were published as articles elsewhere including in other books. I first published "The Wire" in *The Affective Turn: Theorizing the Social*, edited by Patricia Ticineto Clough with Jean Halley (2007). "A Brief History Told in Carpets" came out as "Ranch Style: A History Told in Carpets" in *Qualitative Inquiry*, 11:4 (August 2005). A segment of chapter 3 came out originally in *Seeing White: An Introduction to White Privilege and Race* by Jean Halley, Amy Eshleman, and Ramya Mahadevan Vijaya (2011). I first published "Genealogy: My Family Tumbling Through Time" as "Genealogy: A Tale of Two Families and a Cat" in *Cultural Studies/Critical Methodologies*, 11:2 (2001). Parts of chapter 5 came out as "The Production of Girl Life" in *Qualitative Inquiry and the Politics of Advocacy*, edited by Norman K. Denzin and Michael D. Giardina (2012). Portions of the book, including "Visiting Little America," "This I Know," and "A Special Occasion Dinner" came out originally under the title "This I Know: An Exploration of Remembering Childhood and Knowing Now" in *Qualitative Inquiry*, 6:3 (September 2000). "My Grandmother and the Cleaning Lady" was first published as "The Cleaning Lady: An Exploration of Class and Gender in a Rural Wyoming Family" in *Qualitative Inquiry*, 11:2 (April 2005). Much of chapter 7 came out as "The Death of a Cow" in *Qualitative Inquiry* and *Social Justice*, edited by Norman K. Denzin and Michael D. Giardina (2009). Most of chapter 8 was published originally as "To Speak of My Mother" in *Qualitative Inquiry*, 9:1 (February 2003).

I have needed a lot of help in my life. I am lucky to have, eventually, found it. For this, I owe a great debt to so many. My students have helped me immeasurably to be a better scholar (and better teacher, as well as to simply enjoy life more). At different moments in the life of this manuscript, six of my best students—Tori Felix, Courtney Heiserman, Danielle Lucchese, Kristie Scherrer, Mary Beth Somich, and Shayne Zaslow—were my research assistants. Indeed, Courtney

Heiserman and Shayne Zaslow read and gave rich and detailed feedback on the whole manuscript. The book is significantly improved because of all of these talented young scholars and sociologists. The members of my various writing groups, Grace M. Cho, Rafael de la Dehesa, Hosu Kim, Ananya Mukherjea, Ron Nerio, Melissa Hope Ditmore, Deborah Gambs, Rose Kim, Shari Cohen, Jessie Klein, and Helaine Olen have given me smart feedback, and ongoing encouragement. They were incredibly helpful. I am also very grateful to Rose Kim for generously taking on the task of an additional reading of the entire manuscript. Ron Nerio read several drafts, offered extensive feedback, cried with me once or twice, and encouraged me through it all. Nitza Wilon offered me insightful editorial guidance and advice. Amy Eshleman read and gave me very good feedback on chapter 3. Further, she and Isaiah Halley-Segal generously assisted me in locating a cover image for the book. Norman K. Denzin's encouragement, support, and really, his presence in the world have meant so much to me. The late Janet Spector read the manuscript and was wonderfully, brutally honest in her response. Lore Segal and Beatrice Segal also took the time (in Lore's case, several times over time) to read the entire manuscript and give me detailed, rich, extremely helpful advice as well as so much love. Jacob Segal read the manuscript many, many times and gave me incredibly insightful feedback. If the book is any good, it is in large part due to him.

Patricia Ticineto Clough saw something in me and in my writing. Not only this book, I do not know that I would have published anything at all without her.

It is an awkward thing to thank people for helping one to find one's way into living, so as to make writing this book, and so many other things, possible. This debt cannot be repaid. I do hope Sarah L. Hartman, Richard Holland, Pat Horn, Rakesh Rajani, and Jacob Segal know that I know this.

My closest friends, Richard Holland, Amy Eshleman, Monica Lichtner, Carol Quirke, Quinn Cushing, Janet LeMoal, Ramya Vijaya, Ron Nerio, Wendy Gannett, Kathy Pieper, Sofia Bautista Pertuz, and the late Amy Gateff, and my beloved family, Kathleen O'Malley, Janet Spector, Kate Maxfield, Andrew Maxfield, Sharon Saydah, Sean Maxfield, Joshua Maxfield, Lore Segal, Beatrice Segal, David Segal, Ben Segal, Rakesh Rajani, Maggie Bangser, Amar Rajani-Bangser, and Chhaya Rajani-Bangser gave me so much love and strength. Of course in a book about cows, I must note and express great gratitude to my nonhuman animal companions, all these now deceased—Thomasina, the cat who slept on my neck like a purring electric scarf from when I was five to twenty; Snipaway, my beautiful red horse who twice caught his leg in wire; Dolly, the smart Shetland pony who once ran under a branch just the right height for her to go under and me to go flying; and Jesse, my fat white and gray cat, who slept each night with one paw gently touching me.

My partner Jacob Segal, and my children Isaiah and Lena Halley-Segal make it all, everything I lived through, everything I do, worthwhile.

A Brief History Told in Carpets

My child, Isaiah, knows nothing of carpets. He comes from me; my story is his. And yet, the story, our story, has no place, no time for telling. Life pushes on and he is fully in it. Two years old, he has no room for anything but now. And, anyhow, where Isaiah lives, the floors are wooden. They are old and marked and brown. And because in so many ways, I am like my mother—I too am bad at cleaning—the floors are often dirty. Like my mother, I too, leave the floors collecting the grit and dust and hair of life's passing. Really, the floors don't seem to mind. They, like most of us, make space for what comes, and go on.

Our wooden floors have cracks that run up and down their surface; cracks in-between, lying in the open space amid boards, and cracks within the boards, cracks that snuggle down in the midst of wood like veins. The grit, the grit I inherited from my mother, fills in the cracks, the gaps, the empty spaces in the floor. Actually, at times, it is hard to tell the real floor from the grit, the floor that was meant to be from the floor of life's leavings. It is hard to tell which holds which. It is hard to tell whether the grit is actually the one holding the floor together, rather than the floor holding the grit. Someday, someday maybe, the wood will wear away and the grit will be all that's left, all that is left behind.

Yet, unlike Isaiah, whose dreams began to differentiate themselves from mine on wood, my life has been filled with carpet romance, both fleeting and long-term relationships with carpets. I remember, I remember carpets. Our carpet when I was ten in the rented house on Ord Street was cream, cream shag. And we thought our carpet was a luxury, delicious. It was delicious to sit on the old blue armchair—the only thing I know of that my mother got from the divorce, besides us, her three children, and poverty—lugged from home to home, once velvet, once new, it was delicious to sit on that old blue chair and sink our toes into warm softness, cream shag, wall-to-wall the landlord pointed out.

Then, then, when I was ten, I loved carpets. Only later, in recent years, have I learned to prefer wooden floors; browns and blacks, straight lines and curves, weaving together, mixing chaos with intention. But then, on Ord Street when I was ten, I thought our carpet fancy, elegant, a sign that things were well, even when they weren't. I would spend hours on hands and knees, carefully sweeping that carpet all in one direction like a cream sea. One way, it turned to lighter cream, another way to darker. Did the carpet makers know of this magic, this magic they had made? When I was ten, I would spend hours carefully pushing, sweeping, turning the whole living room to light. And then, and then the carpet became my screen. And I wrote away time on that cream water of my daydreams.

Yet with my love for carpets, like any love, there is always more to tell. There were carpets in all our homes, carpets in my home on Rainbow Street where my mother finally left my father, finally left after ten years of trying. There were carpets in our home on Grand Street, cardboard home on the road out of Grand Junction, at the outskirts of everything, the only home my mother could afford, and even that she couldn't, after my father had us leave his house. Then there was Ord Street, home where we lived with my mother's lover Joe, who was scary and who had two sons, Joey and Chris. Joe's son, Chris, was also scary. We even had carpets in our home on Simon Street, our first home in Grand Junction. There we lived when I was three and my brother five. Simon Street was a Grand Junction-Wyoming-version-of-suburbia home, a home exactly like the homes to its right and left, its front and back. It was "ranch style" in a land of ranches, imitating outer city homes as they imitated Wyoming ranches.

The Simon Street home had carpet that ran wall-to-wall, corner to corner, even up the stairs, short flights of five steps or so into the living room, up again to where the bedrooms waited, down again and down to the television room. That carpet went with you everywhere. You could not leave it behind unless you rushed into the bathroom, where the floor was cheap plastic tile, and quickly, quickly, shut the door. Although, even in the bathroom you could see the carpet reaching, pushing yarn like fingers under the door, following, following you still.

My grandfather bought that house for my father, his son, although my father forgets that. He has a funny way of remembering; it changes the past, and yet in spite of his remembering, somehow, the past as it really was, marks the future still. When my brother asked my father for financial help, my father remembered that his father had never helped him financially. Through this, my father said, his father had taught him the importance of working hard. For this, he would not, could not give or even loan my brother money. He said it would be giving my brother the wrong message.

The house that my grandfather bought for my father was our starter house. And really, in an odd way everything did start there, started and stopped. In this house, the babysitter, who might have been my father's younger brother, and who was really not that young, showed my five-year-old brother and me at three, his penis, pink and poking forward, insistent. I have a feeling kind of memory of knowing, somehow, that this was an event, an event more important than many and less than others, out of all the very striking events of life when one is three and living in the world.

In that house, we had my mother's beloved dog, her favorite dog, *ever* she says, and then forgets, as she admires Milagro, her current dog and also her favorite dog, ever. Tinker was a small black terrier and my mother loved him so, maybe with an intensity deeper, harder than her love for Martin and me. When my mother was in the hospital giving birth to my little sister Annie, the carpet did that dog in. Tinker had an anxiety problem, a problem that led him to pee yellow streams of thick strong smell when my mother, whom he loved, was gone. This upset my father. In my father's mind, dogs were replaceable, carpets cost money, and money was not replaceable. Money had to be held onto, tightly, guarded with a love, a care, a passion even, that might have been admirable had it been directed at another object. Anyhow, my father loved money. And my mother loved her unhappily and appropriately named dog, Tinker. This was one of many reasons the marriage would not, could not ever work. So when my mother went to the hospital to give birth to Annie, my father killed Tinker. And he kept the carpet. He kept it clean, no stains, no stains. And that was that.

Chapter 1

Introduction

This book addresses the intersections of life. I explore the various paths taken to arrive at the now that, once, was my childhood life. Cows and girl, Irish and land, violence and love all found their way to each other, to a moment that is gone but once was and held, for that moment, all of this. In large part, this book is about the meanings of life, girl life and cow life. I explore these meanings by examining the violence that happens to both, the violence, and the trauma that ripples off of violent experience like the tiny cracks in glass that surround the small hole made by a bullet. The hole itself is empty, clear open space. The cracks simply, gently, mark the glass, remaining in it, of it and distinct, all at once.

I use repetition in this book as a means to express trauma. In my memoir writing, repetition happens at the sentence level, the same words said two or three times in two or three sentences again and again. Yet I also repeat scenes, and in particular one scene involving my sister and me, again and again.

As many people who write about trauma or work with traumatized subjects note, trauma often grips the survivor in waves of repetitive experience. Trauma scholar, Cathy Caruth, writes that the traumatic event is "experienced too soon, too unexpectedly, to be fully known and is therefore not available to consciousness until it imposes itself again, repeatedly, in the nightmares and repetitive actions of the survivor." Caruth notes, "Trauma is not locatable in the simple violent or original event in an individual's past, but rather in the way that its very unassimilated nature—the way it was precisely not known in the first instance—returns to haunt the survivor later on."[1]

In this book, I tell only a fraction of the stories of violence in my family. And as one might assume, I changed almost all of the names of people and places. I also altered some events, partly unintentionally because events do get altered in memory, and partly intentionally so as to protect the identities of the people involved. So much happened to people—past and present—around me. Those are not my stories to tell. Yet at the same time, they *are* my stories, for I lived next to, and with, not only the violence but the threat of violence, and of course the pain it inflicted to, on, and in someone close to me, and through them, me. In so many ways, when one of us is harmed, we are all harmed. It is a hard task to decide who owns events, who owns the telling of them, almost as hard as telling itself. For that too, *what happened*, is of course not self-evident.

I end this chapter and start the book with a small and true story about a wire and my horse. The wire, like trauma in my life, holds the horse. It grips tightly. Yet as with all things in life, nothing ever holds anything forever. So this book is a story about being gripped by trauma and it is a story about finding some kind of freedom.

This is also a book about cows. And of course, wire in my rural western childhood was meant to fence in cows. The wire that caught my horse found a cause outside of human intention. It was where it was because, at some point, cows were contained there. Cows acted as a backdrop to my childhood. They were ever present but mundane beings that I saw everywhere. Because they were so present, too present, I usually did not see them at all. For the most part, I doubt they noticed me either. Their story deserves telling too. My grandfather was in the cattle business, so I owe cows a debt. In some part, I must credit my white middle class existence, my life as it is, to beef cows. Like so much of my family history, beef cow history is a violent business. Indeed, there are a number of similarities between the story I tell about my family and the story of US cows.

For the most part, I write the two stories side by side. They are parallel. Yet they are also connected through poststructuralist thought, a body of theory that explores the meaning of life, girl life, cow life, and examines the ways power works through, around, and on all of us. Often, I leave the reader to make other connections, connections involving violence, but also migration, colonization, racism, patriarchy, the land, shifting experiences of time, and life's remarkable push to continue against, if not all, many odds.

Meat: A Mass-Produced Problem

In a Scott Adams *Dilbert* comic strip, Dilbert's dog, Dogbert, is talking with a robot programmed to have the "synthesized shame of every major belief system." The robot says to Dogbert, "I worry … Is it my fault that people get heart attacks?" "No," responds Dogbert, "that's from eating too many cows." It asks, "Is the California drought my fault?" "No," Dogbert answers, "that's from water subsidies to cows." "Global warming?" asks the robot. "Cows again," says Dogbert. "Cows are destroying the earth?" asks the robot. "They're better organized than you'd think," notes Dogbert.[2]

Oddly, given their seemingly moderate intelligence quotient and gentle nature, cows do seem to be at the heart of many global problems today. This reality contrasts sharply with meat industry self-depictions as wholesome and natural: healthy animals being raised on family farms in beautiful rural areas. Exploring the meat industry reveals what cow lives mean.

In this section, I briefly examine the modern industrial meat industry. This industry is the endpoint to the history of cows in the United States, and the story I tell. Most contemporary beef cows exist within the confines of the industrial meat industry.

Of course, some cows are healthy animals being raised on "alternative" farms. The pastoral farm movement offers a small but growing challenge to industrial meat and other industrial food production.[3] Meanwhile, most of our food comes from industrial agriculture. Industrial meat is the fruit of biopolitical engagement with the farm animals we eat. The industrial reality entails profoundly unhealthy animals being raised in filthy and crowded confinement, eating fattening food that they did not evolve to eat. Their deaths are largely routinized, and too often cruelly painful. The ecosystem cannot sustain the immense number of animals produced on factory farms. The waste, alone, that they generate presents a global emergency.[4]

Environmental writer, Daniel Imhoff notes:

> Our domesticated livestock have never been as cruelly confined or slaughtered in such massive quantities in all of history. Every year, at least four domesticated animals are raised for every person on the planet. In the United States alone, nearly 10 billion domesticated livestock—mostly chickens, pigs and cows—are raised and slaughtered annually, a number that is dwarfed if one includes rapidly expanding land- and ocean-based fish farming.[5]

Through the industrialization of breeding, raising, fattening, and killing farm animals on factory farms, we have managed to produce an enormous amount of animal food products. The cost of these mass-produced products *appears* low: many humans now have access to what, in preindustrial times and places, was and what is still considered luxury food. Yet, the *real* costs of factory farming are high and often hidden.

As common practice, factory farm animals experience profound cruelty, and live acutely different lives from those determined by evolution. Imhoff states: "Corporate agribusinesses that have revved the economic engines of the global animal factories have reduced living creatures to mere production units of milk, eggs, and meat. Every step of the way, domesticated animals have been increasingly altered and bred to meet the conditions of their confinement."[6] The Animal Welfare Act of the United States federal government protects animals from cruelty and mistreatment. Yet many people do not realize that the act does not apply to farm animals but only to companion animals (pets) and research and exhibition animals. In contrast, the Humane Slaughter Act protects some factory farm animals (cows but not chickens), and only during their slaughter at the end of their lives. Further, as I discuss in chapter 7, the Humane Slaughter Act is largely ignored in slaughterhouses. Staff attorney, Paige Tomaselli, and former director at the Center for Food Safety, Meredith Niles write, "Horrific animal abuses that could imprison someone if performed on a domestic animal are perfectly legal and acceptable for farm animals."[7]

In a *New York Times* article, Mark Bittman writes about a 19-year-old woman who was charged with a felony and put in jail overnight at Rikers Island for allegedly smashing her sibling's hamster against the floor and killing it. (The charges were later dropped.) Bittman notes,

> Thanks to Common Farming Exemptions, as long as I "raise" animals for food and it's done by my fellow "farmers" (in this case, manufacturers might be a better word), I can put around 200 million male [alive and awake] chicks a year through grinders ... castrate—mostly without anesthetic—65 million calves and piglets a year, breed sick animals ... who in turn breed antibiotic-resistant bacteria, allow those sick animals to die without individual veterinary care, imprison animals in cages so small they cannot turn around, [and] skin live animals ... All of this is legal, because we will eat them.[8]

The problem goes beyond cruelty to animals. For miserably low wages, human workers in the meat industry, many who are immigrants, are in daily and serious danger, on the job. About slaughterhouse wages over a decade ago (and things have only gotten worse), journalist David Bacon writes, "Hourly meatpacking wages had fallen to $4 below the manufacturing average by 1999. The entry-level hourly wage in ConAgra's Omaha plant is $9.20, not much higher than the meatpacking wage of 20 years ago."[9] Workers at concentrated animal feeding operations (CAFOs) endure numerous health problems including respiratory illnesses and repetitive motion injuries. Imhoff reveals, "Studies indicate that at least 25 percent of CAFO workers experience respiratory diseases such as chronic bronchitis and occupational asthma."[10] Workers at US slaughterhouses carry out the most dangerous labor in the nation. Journalist Eric Schlosser notes that when his famous book, *Fast Food Nation*, came out in 2001, "the meatpacking industry had the nation's highest rate of serious injury. It was about three times higher than the national average for factories, despite widespread underreporting of slaughterhouse injuries."[11] Journalist Karen Olsson also observes:

> In 2000 the official illness and injury rate for meatpacking workers was 25 percent. Given the chronic underreporting of injuries in the industry ... the actual injury rate is probably much higher. In Walla Walla, the union examined plant injury logs and found that 781 injuries had been recorded in 1999 and 2000, while in a recent union-sponsored survey of just under 500 workers, two-thirds said they had suffered a work-related health problem in the past twelve months.[12]

In addition to the harm caused to animals and workers, industrial farming is acutely destructive to the environment. Imhoff writes that the foremost cause of deforestation in the Amazon has been to free land for industrial farming of soybeans. The soybeans are grown primarily to feed animals on factory farms. Industrial farms in the United States use "billions of pounds of chemical fertilizer and tens of millions of pounds of pesticides" on their crops "contributing to soil erosion, water pollution problems, and wildlife habitat destruction."[13] Perhaps most shocking—and urgent—is the 2006 United Nations Food and Agriculture Organization report showing that livestock alone accounts for "18 percent of global greenhouse gas emissions, a larger share than all of the world's transportation emissions combined." The World Watch Institute claims that this number is too conservative and maintains instead that livestock causes "51 percent of all greenhouse gas emissions."[14]

Finally, extensive research shows that the animal products generated on factory farms are *also* harmful to those who consume them.[15] Among the health concerns, factory farm meat has high rates of contamination by E. coli 0157, salmonella, and other infectious bacteria.

Imhoff notes, "The Centers for Disease Control and Prevention (CDC) estimate that contaminated meat- and poultry-related infections make up to 3 million people sick each year, killing at least 1,000—figures that are probably underreported." Yet even when the meat is clean, it contributes to the US diet that is high in calories and saturated fat. "According to the Center for a Livable Future at Johns Hopkins University, meat and dairy foods contribute all of the cholesterol and are the primary source of saturated fat in the typical American diet." Studies show that eating large amounts of meat is associated with "obesity and high blood cholesterol ... the leading risk factors for heart disease." Further, because of factory farm feeding practices, the animals likely consume high rates of dioxins and PCBs from pollutants in the environment. Animals store these carcinogens in their fat. Because of rendering practices where factory farm animals are fed the remains of other animals, the pollutants move up the food chain resulting in "a higher concentration of dioxins and PCBs in the animal fats consumed by people."[16]

Michel Foucault on Cows and Girls: For the Theoretically Minded

This is a book about what life means, and how life is valued, cow and gendered human life. My topic is a history of beef cows and the life of my family. In this investigation, I rely on concepts founded by Michel Foucault. Foucault explains that we live in a society where people make choices. He examines how we come to make the choices we make, and the forces involved in influencing us to make those choices. He explores the ways in which these influences do not just operate on us from outside of us. We also internalize them and experience these influences from inside of our own embodied experience. For example, there is immense pressure in our society for girls and women to be thin. US women experience this pressure all around them, for example, in mainstream ideas of what is beautiful and what is ugly, and in popular fitness programs. Women succumb to these pressures, and pressure themselves to be thin. Women watch themselves closely for fault, "do I look fat in this?" and in eating practices where they monitor themselves closely, and in an ongoing way, about how many calories they consume. Foucault calls this process normalization.

Further, Foucault investigates the ways forces such as public health campaigns act on people in large numbers and in a broader way. Public health campaigns against obesity offer an example of biopolitical control and are a counterpoint to women's normalized obsession with thinness. Biopolitical power involves the generalized forces that act upon people rather than the particular influences on people, for example, at home and at work.

In examining the lives of cows, I investigate biopolitics that is the study and manipulation of, in large part through violence against, cow life to more efficiently produce *more* cow, more meat, more profit. Cows' (unpaid) labor is *living*, staying alive as they engorge to the point of bursting, then dying at the hands of humans. In exploring the gendered human lives in my family, I also investigate normalization, that is, the ways in which our gender was inscribed upon us through gendered expectations and labor, and through sexual and other types of violence. Just as beef cows feed humans to reproduce human lives, in the story I tell, girls and women also work to reproduce human lives, also in part, through feeding. Gendered female labor, domestic and unpaid, quietly reproduces biopower. With regard to the links between these two concepts, that is, normalization and biopolitics, Foucault writes:

> In more general terms still, we can say there is one element that will circulate between the disciplinary and the regulatory, which will also be applied to body and population alike, which will make it possible to control both the disciplinary order of the body and aleatory events that occur in the biological multiplicity. The element that circulates between the two is the norm. The norm is something that can be applied to both a body one wishes to discipline and a population one wishes to regularize.[17]

I study biopolitics and normalization through a social history of the American beef industry juxtaposed with my memoir of growing up in Wyoming in the shadow of my grandfather's cattle business. I expose and explore the link between the meat industry and my own experience of the formation of gender and sexuality through family violence. I contrast stories from my childhood with the story of cows, how they came to the United States, how they are raised, how they are slaughtered, and what happens to cows once they are meat. There is a shared history between my family and American beef cows. Fundamentally, both are stories of violence. Both entail migration. Our "founding fathers" came with our founding cows[18] across the ocean. And of course, industrialization acts as a backdrop, or perhaps a motor—driven by human hands—to both, propelling both through time to a funny kind of "progress." In this comparison, I examine contemporary thinking about what life is and what/when/

whose life matters. I study gendered sexual and other violence, and trauma. I am interested in the creation of a docile, but active, human female subjectivity. And I am interested in the unknowable, at least to us humans, subjectivity of cows.

I am also interested in something that is at the edge of my story, and perhaps at the edge of every story, that is, life's potential. Somehow, in the midst of everything, sometimes in the midst of terrible odds, life does, often, go on. In spite of everything, it certainly has for me. And in some way, I do think the trauma I have lived with was a part of that life that pushed me out of violence and into something else. It seems that life pushes for itself. We tend to turn toward the sun.

Mirroring my interest, Nikolas Rose explores Foucault's "fragmentary ideas about aesthetic politics."[19] Rose writes, "Rather than subordinate oneself in the name of an external code, truth, authority or goal, such a politics would operate under a different slogan: each person's life should be its own telos." Drawing from Gilles Deleuze, Rose argues that this politics "would thus have its own minimal normativity: we should oppose all that which stands in the way of life being its own telos."

> This would not be an anthropology or an essentialism of the human: there is no essence here serving as the basis for critique, and waiting to be realized. But perhaps it would embody a certain "vitalism." It would, that is to say, be in favour of life, of the "obstinate, stubborn and indomitable will to live," of the conditions that make possible the challenge to existing modes of life and the creation of new modes of existence.[20]

Biopolitical life, cow life, normalized life, girl life have ends that matter over and above life itself. Yet life has a way of pushing back; indeed, it has a life of its own. For me, this is where hope lies, in the "obstinate, stubborn and indomitable will to live."[21] Just when life seems held so tightly, to the point of having nothing left unto itself, life finds a way out again. It is a tricky thing, life. Thus the trauma I experienced was a response to violence. And perhaps, in that very trauma, lived the way out.

In this book, I engage with theory, particularly feminist materialist, psychoanalytic and poststructuralist thought. Primarily, I express theoretical ideas implicitly in its experimental writing. As noted above, this book rests heavily on, and exists because of, the work of Foucault, his work on normalization, and his recognition and interrogation of biopower or the "technology of power centered on life."[22]

Other contemporary theorists of biopolitics such as Patricia Ticineto Clough[23] and Nicole Shukin[24] also offer an analytic frame for exploring both of the stories I tell, that of my family and the beef industry. I juxtapose these two sites of the production of biopower, cows-becoming-meat, and my family. In my exploration of the meat industry, I burst through a central contemporary (false) binary—human versus animal—to explore not only humans but also other animals.

Ultimately, I expose these stories, of my family, of my grandmothers and me, and of our cows, through and in my experimental writing. I "do" theory in my writing more than explicitly describing or explaining, developing or challenging other theoretical works. The point of my book—my questions and even my arguments—my book's reason for being, is embedded in the storytelling.

Biopolitical questions underlie my investigation of the meat industry and my own violent family: When does life begin and end for the living? When does human life begin and end, distinct from "the animal?" In exploring the relationships between gendered (sexual) violence, and violence against animals, what counts as meaningful life, life to be valued, life to be protected? Whose bodies matter?

Foucault writes that biopower bodes "nothing less than the entry of life into history, that is, the entry of phenomena peculiar to the life of the human species in the order of knowledge and power."[25] For a long time in Europe, political power contained the ability, the right, to allow life or confer death. Yet from the eighteenth century, social theorist Nikolas Rose explains, "political power was no longer exercised solely through the stark choice of allowing life or giving death. Political authorities, in alliance with many others, took on the task of the management of life in the name of the well-being of the population as a vital order and of each of its living subjects."[26] With biopolitics, the state expanded to fulfill its obligations. Yet as Foucault argues, the management of life called forth intellectual and political effort outside of the state "by philanthropists, medical reformers [and] religious organizations."[27] Foucault notes: "The great overall regulations that proliferated through the nineteenth century are, obviously enough, found at the State level, but they are also found at the sub-State level, in a whole serious of sub-State institutes such as medical institutions, welfare funds, insurance, and so on."[28] Biopolitics entail a cultural and political perspective, and address a plethora of human efforts to manage, control, and alter the vital human experience.

In forming and reproducing contemporary social power, biopower works to define both what life entails (and whose life matters) and what death entails. It attempts to, somewhat literally, pin down what it means to be gendered human animal versus other animal—other nonhuman animal, that is, animal supposedly without subjectivity. Philosopher Giorgio Agamben argues that in the seventeenth century, the modern state "began to include the care of the population's life as one of its essential tasks thus transforming its politics into biopolitics, it was primarily by means of a progressive generalization and redefinition of the concept of vegetative life...that the State would carry out its new vocations."[29] Beef cow bodies compile cow populations mattering only for the matter—meat—that their lives produce by living. Cows literally embody capital.

The concept of biopolitics, and Shukin's notion of animal capital discussed below, flows from Foucault's analysis of a type of "governmental reason" found in his critique of German and US neoliberalism. The broader issue is a conception of society defined as the enhancement of life, and this, understood as the development of certain capacities. Neoliberals, in response to the post–World War II Keynesian consensus for a large interventionist government, restate the classical liberal argument for minimal government. About this, Foucault argues that neoliberalism simultaneously claims that it wants government to leave individuals alone, and contains its own governmental reasons. For neoliberals, the market does not need government regulation because markets are regulated by the rationality of competitive individuals pursuing their own self-interest. For Foucault, this thinking assumes individuals are competitive.

Thus, a market society for Foucault is actually an "enterprise society." A particular person fits this society: "The *homo economicus* sought after is not the man of exchange or man the consumer."[30] This person is, in neoliberal thought, an "entrepreneur of himself, being for himself his own capital, being for himself his own producer, being for himself the source of [his] earning."[31] This person fundamentally produces his "own satisfaction." This is achieved to a maximal degree by the amount of "human capital" the person has, which means the person is an "ability–machine." The problem for neoliberals is to build up this capital. For example, in child rearing, this capital is built up in the type of education a child has, the time spent by the parent with the child, the type of conversation engaged in with the child. These are all defined as part of the "problematic" of the development of human capital. Indeed, Foucault notes the time given providing "affection" is an "investment in human capital."[32] For Foucault, problems of public health and hygiene are solved as issues of the development—or loss—of human capital.[33]

Shukin's concept of animal capital is both an extension and a critique of this notion. Shukin addresses Foucault, biopolitics, and in particular, the biopolitical focus on humans. She challenges us to theorize other animals at the heart of the analysis of biopower. She argues, "The biopolitical analyses [Foucault] has inspired ... are constrained by their reluctance to pursue power's effects beyond the production of human social and/or species life."[34] Shukin pushes us to consider the biopolitical making of other animal life—*and* human life as a component of the rest of ("natural") life more generally. She claims, "While theorists of biopower have interrogated the increasingly total subsumption of the social and biological life of the *anthropos* to market logics, little attention has been given to what I am calling animal capital." For Shukin, animal capital is both the economic and the symbolic form of capital that animal lives produce.

Shukin points to a "critical need within the field of cultural studies for work that explores how questions of 'the animal' and of capital impinge on one another within abysmal histories of contingency."[35] Animal capital is produced through both symbolic and material "logics of power."[36] Shukin argues, "The 'question of the animal' exerts pressure on theorists of biopower and capital to engage not only with the ideological and affective function of animal signs but with material institutions and technologies of speciesism."[37]

Shukin offers a model for me in her exploration of biopolitics and animal capital. Drawing from her work, I note that cows—and at times, similarly, girls—are "heavily burdened with a historical complex of economic and libidinal investments." The meaning of cows' lives "vacillat[es] between economic and symbolic logics of power."[38] They hold a central, symbolic place in a national story of origins where the righteous violence of white men (pioneers, mountain men, cowboys) replaces "savage" nature (including in the terms of the story, Native Americans and the "wild") with a uniquely American "civilization." As white people move west and domestic cows replace wild buffaloes, the Wild West is subdued. Cows, like a background to the narrative, hold a quiet yet important place in the story. In comparison, Shukin examines the meaning of beavers in Canadian history. Cows are *symbolically* similar to Shukin's beavers in Canada that

> constitute a powerful nodal point within a national narrative that nostalgically remembers the material history of the fur trade as a primal scene in which Native trappers, French coureurs de bois, and English traders collaboratively trafficked in animal capital, at the same time as

> it advantageously forgets, through the symbolic violence of occupying the semiotic slot of indigeneity, the cultural and ecological genocides of the settler-colonial nation form mediating capital's expansion.[39]

Yet also *economically* similar to beavers in Canada's violent history, cows played a central role in the economic growth of capital across what came to be the United States. Not only did cows make money, lots of money for some, from the cows' flesh and the labor of those who raised, fed, and slaughtered them, beef cows, and the product they embody, meat, offer a model of how economic development happened in the United States. Indeed, historian Jimmy M. Skaggs claims that the meat industry is a "microcosm of American economic development."[40] The story of the meat industry mirrors the story of national economic development. It is a story of white colonization of what became the United States, the interactions between small farmers and developing industrial meat businesses, governmental intervention in and support of businesses small and large, technological development and industrialization, and the national consumption of mass-produced food.[41]

Becoming Cow, Becoming Girl

The treatment of cows reveals what they mean to us. They reproduce power in their increasingly large bodies, and shorter and shorter lifespan. Both the story of US beef and my childhood illuminate the defining and disciplining of contemporary life. What lives mean to us is also revealed in the formation of social norms, as I show in the stories of what it means to be girl in my family, and what it means to be Irish.

Foucault developed the idea of normalization to explain one important way that social power works.[42] In my discussion of the history of my family, I focus on this idea. The framework of this concept, like biopolitics, can be found in Foucault's belief about underlying power structures in liberal society. In *Discipline and Punish: The Birth of the Prison*, Foucault argues that liberalism is purported to be an order of rights, egalitarian and symmetrical relations.[43] However, he argues that what makes this system possible are the inegalitarian and asymmetrical relations of normalization of what he calls the "disciplines" of schools, hospitals, and the other multiplicity of institutions that pervade modern society. Through normalization, individuals are disciplined to be "normal" in a dualistic framework that both springs from and reproduces social power.

Normativity, although not an instrument of those in power according to Foucault, often supports the privilege of the more powerful in society. In the dualism, "normal" defines the supposed attributes—such as being "civilized"—of those in power, those who are predominantly white, male, American, citizens, and middle class. On the other side of this binary, "abnormal" defines the supposed characteristics of marginalized groups, those predominantly of color, female, un-American, undocumented, ethnic, and impoverished. In the dualism, the "abnormal" are understood, for example, as "savage." About this, Jacob Segal writes, "Normalization works through the binary opposition of the normal and the abnormal. The normal becomes the ideal and the abnormal the unthinkable, a division that informs multiplicities of oppositions such as health/sick, straight/gay, sane/mad."[44] Drawing from Foucault, in 2007 I write, "Networks of power operate to support this normalization. By networks of power, Foucault means how power flows through society, and how human beings are both acted upon by power and reproduce it. Through this normalization, we become subjects."[45]

I study the disciplining of girl bodies through violence, as well as the reproduction of biopolitical power in the meat industry. Even at a cellular level in my family, we became gendered and sexual beings through violence. It was like water to a fish, so close we could not see it, know it, realize it, speak it. Ironically, women in my family reproduced power in their increasingly long-lived, smaller and smaller bodies. In my childhood, our beef cows grew fatter and our women grew smaller, frailer. Cows were made to grow large. Girls were made to feel small. My grandmother lived her final years curved over on herself in bed with osteoporosis. In sharp contrast to beef cattle whose short lives revolve around nonstop bingeing, as I remember my grandmother, she did not eat. Yet she—her domestic labor—reproduced the stuff of life day in and day out, repetitively, over and over and over.

So this is my story. Its telling is to force the time I lived, and live, to be complete.

I want to start with my grandmother. Yet how can I tell the story of my grandmother when in some way I never knew her myself. I only have glimpses, moments, and of course, all the ways I did not know her.

And yet, what is it to know someone? Is it to know a list of her traits? Or is it an indescribable sense, an experience one has and comes to have of someone else, that constantly changes? Or is knowing someone simply to share time with her, to be with her in moments of her life? Or is to know someone to own them, and thus, is knowing not really possible?

Knowing a person, a place, knowing what happened, knowing, anything, intrigues me. There were no facts in my family. We lived by rules instead. And if time is three dimensional, as are human beings, we lived in only part of time. Our world had two dimensions. Our world was flat. And truth did not fit there.

The Wire

Caught, you probably know, horses will fight to get free. I know, it sounds simple, silly, or, as an intellectual man I know said, redundant. You probably say, tell me something new. Of course they fight to get free. Still. Still, I find it touching. They will fight to get free, no matter what free means. When a horse gets her leg caught in wire, she will struggle, even as the skin on her leg is peeled all away, even as the wire grips tighter and tighter to her bare bone. It is the nature of a horse caught in wire to fight much as it is the nature of wire caught around the leg of a horse to tighten and grip ever more closely, holding the horse for dear life as though the wire, too, felt desire.

I know about this push, this push from inside, for freedom. Once I held a blade—sharp and even, slender and perfect in its capacity—over my skin. The veins under my freckled pale skin are like my father's. They push out, they push out ready to press on, against, the blade, ready to fight. They are big and bulging, dark blue. And they swirl and swim up and down my arms like ivy. When I was pregnant, the nurses loved me for my veins, with their ready ripeness. Blood comes easy from me. It comes so easy that one time, called from my veins, an inexperienced nurse found herself, and me too, covered in bright red freshness spurting, gushing from the puncture she had made.

Once, feeling the push, the push from inside of me, pressing hard and tight against my ribs and throat, once I held a blade over a deep blue vein in my arm. It was moments from entering, moments from freeing blood to pour, to flood like a Montana river in early spring, out of me. The blade would have let my blood go, finally, rushing free from the confines of my skin and bone around it. It would have filled the bath where I sat, pushed the warm water aside, insisting on its presence, bright and red and thick.

Twice my horse has been caught in wire. The first time he did what horses do. Simply, he fought. He fought and the wire tightened and held ever more closely to him. It gripped around his bone, ungiving. Bone offers a match for wire that skin cannot meet. Thick and tough as horsehide is, it yields to wire, opens soft and smooth like petals, ready. My beautiful red horse fought the wire and it held tighter and tighter and sliced as deep, as far as it could. His bone offered real resistance. The wire began to work on the bone and my horse wet and exhausted struggled more. Given time, I am sure the wire would have won. In a sense at least, in a sense, the wire would have won. But then again, the tables would have turned had the wire had time to work its way slowly through the bone of my horse's leg. The tables would have turned because, once through, once through horsehide and bone, the wire would find only itself, again. And my horse, my horse would have been free.

Yet, it did not come to that. We found my horse, my horse caught in wire, his leg drenched in red. We found my horse before the wire had a chance to work its way back, though my horse, to itself. The vet said I had to put my horse down. But I didn't. I kept him still for days to see if the flesh could find its way back together, meeting, joining, lumpy, and hard. The vet said it would not heal. But what is healing anyhow. The flesh did find its way to itself, and it covered the naked leg bone in an awkward sort of way. My horse limps still, as though the memory of that wire holds him, even now, tightly.

Somehow life pushes for itself. It demands. It demands freedom. I know, I know it pulsing inside of me. I know it pushing, up my throat like vomit, pushing, insisting, pressing the breath from me. I imagine the relief of that breath let go. I imagine the relief of red flooding everywhere filling all that emptiness, pushing out under through emptiness to something else. I imagine myself melting body into body, rotting flesh and bone into soil and root and other flesh. Finally free.

My friend Erin pushed herself, material into material. She set herself free to become, into, something else. My friend Erin used to sit in the bath the door closed as tightly as doors will close and you know nothing ever shuts anything out for good. Erin used to sit in the bath and listen to her mother's husband talk to her through the door. His voice cut through to her. He wanted to see her, be her, feel her young girl body, naked in the bath.

One day Erin told someone. And because she was causing a disruption of course they removed her from the home. She lived in foster care for a year until her body learned to control itself. Until her body quit asking her stepfather to stand outside the bathroom door. No one ever knew if removing the body worked to bring rest to the disruption. Finally Erin's drunk mother got rid of her drunk husband and they figured they might as well let Erin go home. She could not cause any more trouble at that point anyhow.

Erin did go home. She allowed herself to fall and fall and fall, until she came to earth. She came matter to matter, body to body.

The impact was noisy, a smacking of flesh on flesh. Her body burst inside, not out. Somehow the skin held everything together. But the insides of Erin burst, exploded pushing, merging, changing everything forever. The skin held tight, firm, resolved. Not a bit of Erin leaked anywhere. At least not then. Because, eventually, even skin, even wire has to let go.

Twice my horse caught his leg in wire and wire caught my horse. The second time, I was riding him. I felt his body go taut beneath me. And I held him back, vomit rising in my throat, I held my horse. Still, I said. He and I quivered there together. If my horse went wild, wild like letting go as I jumped down from him, if my horse went wild, he could throw me hard to the ground. Leaping thrashing for freedom, my horse could so easily push and tangle me under him amidst wire and earth and hard sharp horse hoof. Still I said shaking as my hand felt its way down the tense leg of my horse, felt its way down through deep winter coat, dusty and warm. My hand bumped, cold, thin, human skin against even colder, even thinner so hard wire in the midst of thick horse fur. I met the wire there.

I know desire. I know desire. I too want freedom. I feel its push inside of me, pushing out up my throat, pushing pulsing. I want. Relief.

Maybe it is in my blood this push to leave skin and bone behind, this particular push for freedom. This longing to die. My mother and her mother too seemed to long this way. My mother ate a thermometer when she was four. They had told her about the mercury inside, beautiful silver stuff, moving like magic through the thin glass stick. She knew that mercury was to be admired from behind the safety of glass. So longing, longing, she shattered the glass, setting mercury free. She called it inside herself, longing. It is a funny kind of push. It is a funny kind of push, for life, for life.

And my grandmother stayed with my grandfather. She stayed tempting his desire. Maybe her staying was also this longing called into living, this longing to be free. Maybe staying she hoped that somehow, someday his beating would break through and release her.

Oh, how I long to be free. Let me go let me go let me go let me go let me go. I long to be free. I imagine. Falling, falling falling. Erin's friend said she was laughing when she fell. She fell free. She fell. And I too long to be free.

Chapter 2

Where the Cows Came From

We have examined the general framework of biopolitics. In this chapter, I take up Shukin's challenge to cross the species barrier and consider more life, nonhuman animal life, in theorizing the "technology of power centered on life." In terms of animal capital, American cows embody *both* iconic symbols of American-ness *and* the material production of capital through their bodily matter. The material of cow produces capital. And the symbol of cow, the sign, the representation, also produces capital. In this chapter, I suggest that cows play a pivotal role in a central (and binary) story of white American origin, that is, the white male conquest of the American West, *cow*boys (a word that notes the important relationship between animal and gendering-human), Indians, and the winning out of "civilization" over "savage" wilderness.

This story of civilization produces masculinity as well as girl-ness. In the story, watching from the margins, girls and women play the role of witness. They are the story's recipients; they catch and hear and see the story. And by this, they make the story "real." (White) men become men. Animal lives and human lives of color are supposedly subdued. "Civilization" is born.

Animal capital is produced in part through violence; violence is a technology of power. Violence, of course, is not a thing, person, or animal. It is a movement, an action, a force that leaves in its wake altered states. Violence brings about change. And not all violence is equal. This has as much to do with the violated as the violent action. Even though children, cats, and cows all feel pain, the same violent act performed on a cow is considered acceptable, and not on a cat or a human child. One can hang a cow upside-down by one leg and slice open its neck, but in the United States, performing the same action on a cat (or a child) would be unacceptable and by some interpretations of the law, even illegal, although the material reality, the cells altered, the movement of metal against and in flesh, is quite similar in each case.

It was late at night. And we were little girls. My sister even smaller than I. My sister loved that cat. She loved that cat. Really, she had not much else to love. And he woke us up. And he brought us to the garage. I don't remember getting there. Instead, suddenly, in my mind, it is night and we are there, my sister and I, standing side by side. Our backs are to the door, the door out of the garage, the door to the house, the door through which we must have just come. Through this door, one finds the stairs dropping down, down to where our bedroom waits. My sister and I stand, our backs to the door, our feet bare on cold, cold with the night, cement. We face my father. As always, we do as he says. We watch. We were in our nightgowns, two small girls, very small. And he took that cat. My sister's cat, all black, soft and sleek, went everywhere with her. Drunk, my father took that cat.

I am a man he told us.

And, he sliced that cat right down the middle.

He gutted my sister's cat. And we watched, late at night, in our nightgowns, in the garage.

In what follows, I present a brief history of white conquest and the role of American beef cows, beef ranching, and the beef industry in it. I also examine popular ideas about cows, cowboys, and "the frontier" such as is found in the work of Frederick Jackson Turner.[1] I investigate the "realities" of these entities in contrast to the powerful, quintessential American myths about them. About this history, Patricia Nelson Limerick argues: "Like slavery, conquest tested the ideals of the United States. Conquest deeply affected both the conqueror and the conquered, just as slavery shaped slaveholder and slave. Both historical experiences left deep imprints on particular regions and on the nation at large. The legacy of slavery and the legacy of conquest endure, shaping events in our own time."[2] Interestingly, as Limerick points out, these two experiences play different roles in mainstream American memory.

The frontier represented instrumentality in place. The frontier *signified* a place of becoming, becoming something more, something better than whatever one had been. In the popular imagination, the value—and the power—of the frontier grew from the future possibilities that the mainstream believed it held.[3]

Like the frontier, cows, indeed their very flesh, played an important role in American history, including its supposed progress and development. In fact, the animal itself embodies shifts in the human societies that feed on it. Preindustrial cows lived cow lives truer to cow evolution, grazing on the food they evolved to eat, grass, and growing to be a cow-size their bodies had evolved to be (rather than the obese size beef cows become today). Further, most healthy preindustrial cows lived more years than their beef counterparts today, and did what bovine animals do with their time when left to their own devices: graze. Depending on the type and lifestyle of the cows, their lifespans range from 15 to 25 years. Nonetheless, humans have usually killed them while they were still young, before their meat became too tough. By the early twentieth century, beef cows were regularly killed for slaughter at four or five years of age. In the 1950s, slaughter occurred at two or three years. By the end of the twentieth century, beef cattle could expect to live from 14 to 16 months.[4]

The first cows, preindustrial cows, came to the United States much like my Irish predecessors did, on boats, although the cows came earlier than most Irish. Both cows and Irish were migrants, one choosing to migrate, if one can choose anything when living in and trying to leave behind extreme poverty. The other, the cows, did not choose. They just came, arriving early on in US history, many during colonial times. And they came with other farm animals. Colonists traveling to Jamestown in 1607 brought cattle, pigs, sheep, poultry, goats, and horses as living provisions on the boat, the *Susan Constant.* Unfortunately for the provisions, famine led the colonists to kill and eat all of the nonhuman animals during their first winter.[5] These were some of the first but not the last cows to travel to North America.

In 1611, and over the years, more cows and other animals traveled to the colonies. To ensure a future for them, to ensure that they reproduced, Sir Thomas Dale ordered that the 1611 animals be protected.[6] And given that protection, reproduce they did. This was good because, whereas English supply ships continued to regularly bring more livestock to the colonies, often only half of the animals on a given ship made it through the journey alive. Sometimes even more than half were lost. The seas were rough, the ships were overcrowded, and they frequently did not carry enough feed. And the lost half was small to begin with because the ships were little in the 1600s. They could only carry a small number of animals.[7]

In spite of the small numbers, colonialists were not protective of their livestock. Early cattle ranching in the United States was a hands-off affair. Cows, along with horses and pigs, roamed free. They lived in the woods near each colonial settlement, finding their own food, breeding, and making lives for themselves. Only sheep required human labor, since only sheep, being neither smart nor industrious, needed active human care to survive. The others lived wild lives, preyed upon by wolves and snakes. Native Americans also killed and ate them. And of course the colonists consumed them. In spite of these ever-present threats, the cows reproduced and even thrived. Skaggs writes, "In 1627 estimates placed 5,000 cattle in Virginia; twenty years later 20,000 cattle, 3,000 sheep, 5,000 goats, 200 horses, and 50 asses were counted in the colony. In those days enumerations ignored all classes of farm poultry and even swine, which were so numerous as to be considered pests by many settlers."[8]

In Massachusetts among other places, cows wandered about human villages, passing time. Cows literally marked our lives through the paths they made, paths that became streets in cities like Boston.

Cows also became living markers between white, "civilized" colonial settlements, and "wild" Native land. Cows existed on the borders of white lives and became the living presence that signaled white movement west, and further west again. As the white settlers cleared land of woods and turned it into farms, cow herders moved further west looking for places to graze their cattle. And again the settlers would become too many for their current land. Some moved west once more and cleared more land, pushing cow herders further west again to graze their cattle on the *new* frontier. Rather than the pioneers, rather than the white, Indian-fighting cowboy, the not-so-gallant, not-so-brave cow was the real "hero" of the colonizer's frontier. It was cows that actually pushed that limit slowly west.

The frontier-as-cow made a border between the supposedly civilized and those deemed uncivil. And that frontier, both in reality and in the American imagination, played a central role in American "development." In 1893, historian Frederick Jackson Turner spoke about this in his famous lecture, "The Significance of the Frontier in American History." While it was published later, Turner first gave his lecture at the 1893 World's Fair, the World's Columbian Exposition in Chicago, to a group of historians. Turner picked the perfect place to talk about conquest. The fair was organized to commemorate and celebrate the legacy of Christopher Columbus and the four hundredth anniversary of his expedition.[9]

Turner argued that the frontier was that between what we once were, and what we have and will become. The frontier, claimed Turner, was always at the "outer edge of the wave—the meeting point between savagery and civilization."[10] For Turner, being from the United States, being (white) "American" was a becoming that happened through this encounter of civilized *man*—of course—with the wild and uncivilized edge that exists on the other side of "us." Perhaps more than anything else, mainstream Americans become through this myth making, imagining ourselves into being through stories, fantasies about what others are and we are not.

Mainstream ideas about masculinity were at the core of this fantasy. Indeed, in this framework, civilization's ever-changing "outer edge" birthed masculinity through its violent movement of so-called progress. In this thinking, masculinity came from, was born out of conquest, the masculine became masculine through conquering, subduing, controlling, entering Others.

And he woke us up. And he brought us to the garage. I don't remember getting there. Instead, suddenly, in my mind, it is night and we are there, my sister and I, standing side by side. My sister and I stand, our backs to the door, our feet bare on cold, cold with the night, cement. We face my father. As always, we do as he says. We watch.

Real men could never be submissive, never be entered, but only actively move forward, entering others, entering the conquered. In the case of the frontier, the normative white and male, heterosexual, young, and "civilized" conquered the "savage," the natural, the earth, the feminine, and the animal in (and of) the American West.

This idea, Turner's frontier thesis, plays a seminal role (so to speak) in the mainstream United States. Turner's argument helped to formulate a popular idea, a story, myth, fantasy that "we" are a people who engage with the "wild" and become more, more than what we were, through that engagement. Of course, a lot of people are left out of this "we." Moreover, the ideas did not come out of nowhere; conquest really happened.

Conquest really happened. And with it, the ideology of conquest shaped the thinking that lived in and around the domination of the West, of western Native people, and of western land and other resources. In this thinking, conquest birthed a uniquely American "civilization." The actual experiences of conqueror and conquered were a somewhat different story.

Limerick writes, "To most twentieth century Americans, the legacy of slavery was serious business, while the legacy of conquest was not."[11] Limerick continues, "Southern historians successfully fought through the aura of moonlight and magnolias, and established slavery, emancipation, and black/white relations as major issues in American history ... Conquest took another route into national memory."

Growing up in a small and predominately white town in Wyoming in the 1970s, the children I knew never played masters and slaves. However, we *did* regularly play "cowboys and Indians." And we never received toys representing the social relations of southern slave society. We did get "cowboy and Indian" toys. These came in a standard variety of forms. There were costumes to be worn representing the two sides of this colonial history. There were toy guns, and toy bows and arrows. There were little plastic pieces, usually solid in color, often forest green or brown. Half of these were cowboys with cowboy hats and boots and guns, riding horses using western saddles. Half were Indians, always men, mostly naked carrying bows and arrows, riding horses bareback. In the games and in the broader framework of our historical understanding, inevitably, the Indians were the bad *guys*, the backward ones, noble at best, dirty and cruel at worst. And of course, the cowboys were the good *guys*. There were no women or girls. And we all knew, somehow, that for white women either you were a lady or you were dirty, bad. It never occurred to us to play at being Bad Girls, whores, anymore than it occurred to us to play at being slaves.

Limerick writes, "In the popular imagination, the reality of conquest dissolved into stereotypes of noble savages and noble pioneers struggling quaintly in the wilderness ... The subject of slavery was the domain of serious scholars and the occasion for sober national reflection; the subject of conquest was the domain of mass entertainment and the occasion for lighthearted national escapism."[12]

In our play, we took our cues from the westerns that I grew up periodically watching at the movie theatre (single screen, and the only one in town) on Saturday afternoons. I remember eating candy and watching the brave acts of courageous white men fighting for "what's right." I do not remember understanding what that was, what *was right*, just that that was what the courageous cowboys fought for, time and again. The fact that nearly everything was *wrong* in my life, and all that was hidden, only made the two-dimensional screen where the movie's story played that much thinner, and perhaps a little easier to burst through when finally I began to push the edges of accepted truths in my own family.

Through conquest, white non-Jewish European immigrants and Anglo-Saxon Americans became men, unless of course they were women. Women did not become anything. And again, the men were men because of action taken to conquer the wild, that is, *violent* action. American studies scholar Richard Slotkin writes, "'Progress' itself was defined in different ways." Yet in every formation, "the Myth of the Frontier relates the achievement of progress to a particular form or scenario of violent action."[13] Without violence, the European immigrant men remained children at best, and effeminate (gay) adults at worst.

> And he took that cat.
> I am a man he told us.

The mainstream American fantasy does bear some resemblance to the American reality (albeit probably not what Turner was thinking). Really, everyone, everyone is always transformed, always changed by their encounter with the edge of themselves.

And when it comes to cows, they actually do change us as we encounter them. They are the animal edge, the frontier that we incorporate into us. We devour them and they transform our bodies anew. The cows quite literally become something more, something else. They become us.

Again, this is probably not what Turner had in mind. Turner was talking about development and "progress." And he conceived of progress in the United States in a manner that continues to be the norm. Turner framed the frontier, framed our normative culture in a way that still resonates. Indeed, contemporary historian, John Mack Faragher called Turner's lecture on his frontier thesis, "the single most influential piece of writing in the history of American history."[14] It is understood—progress, the frontier moving west, the wild becoming civil, and the American spirit born out of this encounter—as both a good and an inevitable thing. Turner almost certainly never thought about progress from the cow's perspective.

> I am a man he told us.

In the violent story that I tell, my father's family made it, became wealthy, off of the backs of cows, and of course, off of the unpaid labor of women in my family. Cows, and ultimately American economic development, worked for them, worked, that is, depending on how one defines "working." In the midst of the mess that bodies make, lives bumping up against one another, violence opening the bodies like wire cutting through the leg of a horse, so that we bled together a bit, blurred and changed, in the midst of all that, they became wealthy. And they believed all of the stories too, stories of progress, stories of civilization built, stories of the strength of strong men and the purity of good women, stories of the simplicity of and danger presented by Indians, Black folks and other people of color, stories of how the righteous and right always won out in the end. For my family, the good guys did well in life. The bad guys did poorly. So you could see how someone was doing, and thus know what kind of a person she was, all at once.

Dreams of the Past

And the basement went on and on and on, halls and rooms, tunnels curving here, winding there. It unfolded back, and again back in time, through years, then more years. And all the while, menace pressed in on us like a hand, reaching. It was always almost there, always almost grabbing hold, lurking panting pushing in on us like a bad horror movie. Danger pushed against the windows that kept appearing in my mind. I was afraid. And how many ways are there to say it. I was afraid. I tried to find a place where we could rest, the we that we were, always, changing. Yet most important, my child, my son, my love kept slipping out of my reach. And then, I became the hand, only frantic, edging against panic, stretching to locate him again, stretching to enclose him against, in, within me. In the dream I tried to find a place where we could rest. And I made resting places on the way, as we ran on through time and basements of my past woven together reaching across spaces, places too large to ever really cross. Finally, I made a bed in a cement and unfinished basement room. I made a bed on the floor from sofa mattress pads, old blankets, and memories and things. I tucked my child in. To sleep, my child, to sleep amidst my fear. As the basement ran on, around us.

Chapter 3

Where the Irish, Where My Family, Came From

I would like to burrow back in time and locate a beginning to my own history, to my family's story of violence. It is as though finding the beginning would free my family from our sadness, from what looks, in looking back, like fate. Still, it is impossible to know how anything, really, started. Moving back, through the story time tells, one finds oneself stumbling further and further away into more and more distant beginnings, beginnings that are someone else's endings.

So, unable to offer it to myself, I cannot give you, my reader, a beginning to, or an answer for, my story. I can only try to offer you, and me, some sense of where the characters in my story—the animals, the Irish, my family—come from, some sense of how and why we came to this moment, now, in the particular and sometimes terrible way we did.

My personal experience of violence and my attempts to understand my family's suffering have been profoundly disorienting. In turn, I present some of my social and family history in a way that I expect will disorient you, my reader. In particular, the below genealogy, with its flood of names, may be confusing. I intend for us both, you and I, for a moment, to be carried away, for a moment to become a little bit lost.

I am interested in looking backwards at the origins of things. How did we come to be who we are in my family, so violent, so afraid? How did we become white and middle class and "American"? How did we come to be in the United States and so poor upon our arrival? How did we come to be so very sad?

Like many other Irish immigrants during and following the Potato Famine, my Irish ancestors came to the United States seeking to escape poverty through the new jobs industrialization offered. In this migration, the Irish changed more than their geographic location. As historian Noel Ignatiev explains, when the Irish first emigrated from Ireland, they were one race, Irish.[1] Over the ensuing century, they shifted from Irish to white. In a process named by Foucault as normalization, the Irish immigrants changed in manifold other ways including from Irish to American, immigrant to citizen, oppressed to dominant and mainstream. We have already discussed the general concept of normalization in chapter 1. Here we see how normalization operates in the history of the Irish in the United States. In becoming white, in becoming American, Irish immigrants went through a process of normalization.

My Irish American family took part in this transformation, including to whiteness—a transformation that dramatically influenced the developing Irish American cultural identity. Becoming white in the United States has meant a denial of white violence. Whiteness entails a washing away from white consciousness the violent/violated realities of many peoples' lives.

Stepping backwards even further, before looking at this Irish American example of the process of normalization, I want to examine what brought the Irish to the United States, the economic forces and types of domination that existed in Ireland, and in the world.

Ireland, Potatoes, and the "Modern World System"

Most Irish Americans look back to a distant agrarian past. In the nineteenth century, before my family immigrated to the United States, the majority of Irish in Ireland was Catholic and lived as peasants. Deeply disempowered, they subsisted as poor and landless farmers in a feudal society. They paid much of the crops they produced as rent to landowners who were neither poor nor Irish Catholic. Although they grew and raised many things, the Irish Catholic majority ate potatoes. Indeed before the Potato Famine, three million of Ireland's population of about eight million depended on potatoes for their day-to-day subsistence. In contrast to stereotypes, this was not, of course, because the Irish had a natural, biological need for potatoes. Rather, potatoes were nutritious, filling, and easy to grow. Other crops, crops more desirable to elites, went to the landlords.

In the sixteenth century, while Europeans began to travel west across the Atlantic Ocean, potatoes came east, to Ireland from the Andes Mountains in Peru. Both Europeans and potatoes moved as parts of the Modern World System that began in the mid-fifteenth century when Europeans "discovered" areas of Africa, Asia, and the Americas and the resources they held.[2] Drawing from the work of

Immanuel Maurice Wallerstein, historians Ewen and Ewen write, "The flourishing of a 'Modern World System,' driven by exploration and mercantile trade, obliterated many of the customary boundaries that had previously separated people from one another."[3] Wallerstein saw the Modern World System as an economic order that, for the first time, encompassed most of the globe. What this system meant was the exploitation of large areas of the world (the "periphery") by Europe (as Europe came to be what Wallerstein called the "center").[4] The lives of the Irish, along with peoples across the world, were profoundly altered by this new system.

European empire and early capitalism crept around the globe. And in the reverse direction, luxury goods from other continents began to pour into Europe "feeding the insatiable appetites" of the European aristocracy. Ewen and Ewen note, "The merchant class, whose wealth was built on such exchanges, followed the social lead of aristocrats and emerged as a prime consumer of luxury items."[5] In this newly interconnected world, Europe developed as a powerful region by exploiting the labor and resources of other areas.

Wealth flowed into Europe vis-à-vis its position in the Modern World System. In Europe itself the "enclosure" movements played an important role in the development of European capitalism. Particularly in Western Europe, land that had once been used for growing crops to feed local populations was now used as enclosed pasture for sheep and cattle. By the sixteenth century, the enclosure movements turned "previously accessible common lands into fenced-in property." The enclosed land housed the sheep that produced the material necessary for the new textile industry that, in turn, funded the growing exchange economy.[6] With the land they once farmed enclosed and cut off from them, peasants and other rural people flooded the rapidly growing cities searching for means of survival. The enclosures created a food shortage. Ewen and Ewen write, "Amid an impending crisis, Western Europe began looking elsewhere for food."[7] Eastern Europe became a source of grain for Western Europe. "Concurrently, relations between Western Europe and other parts of the world became entwined as never before." European colonies in the Americas supplied sugar to feed the European urban masses. Indigenous populations on multiple continents were uprooted, forced into laboring for the colonizers, and in some cases, brutally and "entirely eradicated."[8] Ewen and Ewen explain:

> The densely populated western coast of Africa soon became the source for a much needed labor supply. Beginning in the sixteenth century, millions of souls were drawn into an expanding web of empire,

transported across the ocean, and bound into the modern system of plantation slavery to make money for the European merchants and to feed a population that could no longer adequately feed itself.[9]

The Penal Laws

Ireland played its own tiny role in the global drama, becoming a colony of England in the sixteenth century in the same time period that the potato made its debut in Ireland. Ireland remained a colony under England for centuries, and by about 1750, Irish Catholics owned only 7 percent of their own national land.[10] This is a problem when one lives within an agrarian and subsistence economy.

As a colony, the Irish lived under English rule and England controlled all Irish resources. The English had an aristocratic relationship to the Irish peasants. By the late seventeenth century, Irish Catholics lived under a group of English regulations called the Penal Laws—a variety of codes imposing a dualistic racial and class hierarchy on Irish Catholics and regulating most facets of their lives, including public, family, and religious life; lives, most likely, led in desperate poverty.[11]

The Irish, of course, are no more a race than any other group of human beings. Race is an idea born out of culture and normalization. As described by Ignatiev, outside of the cultural labels regarding race "and the racial oppression that accompanies them, the only race is human."[12] The Irish, or more specifically, the Irish Catholics that I come from, have lived under and with a variety of ideas about race and oppression. When my family and other Irish Catholics immigrated to the United States in the mid-1800s, "they were fleeing caste oppression and a system of landlordism that made the material conditions of the Irish peasant comparable to those of an American slave."[13] The material conditions were the concrete circumstances of their lives; that is, most Irish lived in dire poverty as peasant farmers on land they did not own and paid a large portion of their crops for the "right" of use.

According to Ignatiev, in the eighteenth century my Irish Catholic ancestors living under the Penal Laws were not allowed to:

Vote;
Serve in Parliament;
Hold public office in any of the municipal corporations;
Live within the limits of incorporated towns;
Practice law;
Hold a post in the military or civil service;
Teach in a school;

> Open a school; . . .
> Attend the university;
> Educate their children abroad;
> Manufacture or sell arms, newspapers, or books;
> Own or carry arms;
> Own a horse worth more than five pounds;
> Take on more than two apprentices (except in the linen trade);
> Be apprentices to Protestants;
> Rent land worth more than thirty shillings a year;
> Lease land for longer than thirty one years; [or]
> Make a profit from land of more than one third of the rent paid.[14]

Further, the English as Protestants worked to solidify their power by marginalizing Catholicism. They forced Catholic bishops to leave Ireland and never return or to face the death penalty, and barred new Catholic priests from entering the country. They allowed one Irish Catholic priest to practice in each parish as long as they always stayed at their parish, only leaving with special permission.[15]

As in other colonial situations—many of those others also British—Britain did not do the work of being a colonial power on its own. Middlemen were effective tools of colonization. Below the British but above Irish Catholics in Ireland, were "the Dissenters." These Dissenters, "who were mostly Presbyterian farmers, mechanics, and small tradesmen," descended from English soldiers and from Scots who settled in Ireland, helped maintain the oppressive hierarchy imposed by Britain.[16] They saved the British labor and trouble, often receiving relatively little in return. They did gain one important benefit from their social position. Like Irish Catholics, they themselves might live in terrible conditions, but as Protestants, they could at least consider themselves part of the dominant—the better, the normative—race. In other words, in terms of their "race," all Protestants benefited from the British-imposed hierarchy. No matter how poor they might be, Protestants gained a normalizing psychic power from being Protestant Irish, and not Catholic.[17]

The Potato Famine

Ireland was, in the words of writer Terry Golway, "a country of landless peasants and farm laborers who worked fields they did not own and raised crops they could not eat."[18] The crops included wheat, oats, and barley. Irish peasants also raised livestock such as pigs, cows, sheep, and chickens. These crops, as well as the livestock, thrived in abundance; they thrived, even in the worst years of the infamous

Potato Famine. How strange for my Irish ancestors, in the midst of a famine when at least one out of every eight Irish died, to have enough food all around, and to have grown this food through their own backbreaking labor, and to starve in spite of this.

The issue was not a lack of food. The issue during the Potato Famine was power—and powerlessness. Robert Kee, a British historian and journalist, noted the profuse amounts of food shipped for profit by the landowners in Ireland on one day during the Potato Famine, November 18, 1848. On that single day in the middle of a famine that killed at least a million Irish, "147 bales of bacon, 120 casks and 135 barrels of pork, 5 casks of hams, 300 bags of flour, 300 head of cattle, 239 sheep, and 542 boxes of eggs" were shipped from Cork out of the country.[19] Ireland was an agricultural exporter sending food to feed wealthier people in wealthier lands. Irish farmers did not benefit from this system. They only grew the food from which the English colonizers profited. Golway writes that Irish immigrants to the United States, years later, told their children, children born in this new land, "of the sight of food convoys under armed guard making their way past hollow-eyed men, women, and children whose mouths were green from eating grass."[20]

Through the six years of the Potato Famine, the English who ruled Ireland believed—like many conservatives in the United States today—that no one should hinder the supposedly natural movement of "free" trade and the "free" market. Most of the food in Ireland (all except the potato) was grown for export. And so, export it they did. The relatively wealthy landowners in Ireland as well as the British government depended on the exporting of these crops to maintain their powerful position and wealth. The ideology of a "free" market supported the reality of their power.

However, "free" trade thinking only extended as far as these landowning elites needed it. At the time of the famine, elite British landowners and farmers in England benefited from a decidedly anti-free market set of protections called the Corn Laws, passed into law in 1815 and repealed in 1846.[21] The Corn Laws were government-sanctioned high taxes on imported corn and other grains. They protected British landowning aristocrats and farmers who grew grain from non-British competition. The Corn Laws allowed the British to charge enormously high prices for British corn. Actual free trade would have lowered the cost of grain, making bread and grain available to the Irish, averting the famine.

British greed sat at the heart of the famine, but British ideology held that the real problem sprang from Irish character, from something inherent in their supposed race. In this normalizing dualism, British elites are "normal" and Irish Catholics "abnormal." In this framework, Irish political economic suffering springs from their abnormal position rather than from British oppression. Charles Trevelyan, appointed by the British prime minister to oversee relief operations in Ireland during the Potato Famine, wrote about the Irish, "The great evil with which we have to contend [is] not the physical evil of famine, but the moral evil of the selfish, perverse and turbulent character of the people."[22] Golway observes,

> The goal of British policy, then, was not simply to feed people but to transform their character, to make them something other than Irish. For virtuous Victorians, famine and death in Ireland were yet another reflection of Irish morals and values, so unlike those of British politicians.[23]

The one variety of potato that came to Ireland in the sixteenth century turned out to be extremely vulnerable to fungus. Albeit unknown when it struck during the Potato Famine, the fungus, *Phytopthora infestans,* caused the potato plant's leaves to turn black. The infected potato itself rapidly decayed "into a kind of sugar, producing a putrid, inedible meat."[24] Golway notes that when a "mysterious blight had appeared after a wet summer in 1845 ... newspapers reported with barely concealed fear that the disease had laid waste to potato beds literally overnight."[25] Golway quotes a contemporary newspaper from 1845 when the famine began:

> "In one instance the [farmer] had been digging potatoes—the finest he had ever seen—from a particular field ... up to Monday last; and on digging in the same ridge on Tuesday he found the tubers blasted, and unfit for the use of man or beast," the Dublin-based *Freeman's Journal* reported.[26]

No one was prepared for the next six years in Ireland. The potato crops suffered the disease, year after year from 1845 to 1851, and the loss of crops was immense. For example, in 1846, the crop produced only 20 percent of the amount grown before the famine.[27] The loss of human lives was, also, vast. In 1841, Ireland's population was 8.1 million. By 1851 it was 6.5 million. Compared to its historical pattern of population growth, it should have reached about 9 million people by that year. Ireland's population continued to drop for decades. By the end of the twentieth century it was 5 million, making Ireland the single country in Western Europe that had "fewer people in the 1990s than it had in the early 1840s."[28] The figures vary. Yet most believe that during the six-year famine, Ireland lost one million to immigration and one million to death.

Many died from starvation. Many others died from diseases related to famine and severe poverty. One such disease was typhus, or what people called "road fever." It thrived especially in places where the starving poor were crammed together, such as in workhouses, the English alternative to charity. In the workhouses, people in need worked for their living, if one could call it that. In truth, workhouses were only marginally preferable to death, and many met their death in them. In workhouses, families were split up. Each person did whatever work the government assigned him or her. Often men broke stones, women knitted, and children trained in industrial labor.[29] Working too hard, and living in extremely tight quarters with too many starving people, disease spread rapidly. Records show that some "workhouses produced more than a hundred corpses a week."[30]

Death in Ireland was everywhere. There were not enough coffins to keep up with its staggering pace, and people began employing a reusable model. It had a trapdoor at the bottom so that the corpse could be carried in dignity to the grave. Once there, the trapdoor was opened and the corpse was placed in its bed. The living returned the coffin to be used again. Many could not even afford this inexhaustible type of coffin. Many simply covered their dead in straw.[31] And the horror went on and on. Golway writes:

> The place where the first Famine death was recorded soon became so overrun with the dead and dying that even 150 years later, its name is linked with starvation. Skibbereen was the Famine's ground zero, a place of such horror that British relief officials could scarcely believe their eyes. Letters dispatched to London recorded the awful conditions: A man, barely alive, on the roadside with his three dead children lying next to him; dozens of bodies half-consumed by rats; a wraith-like woman, hollow-eyed, standing in a field.[32]

Most Irish Catholics, then and now, understood that the British were responsible for the famine. Many remain deeply angry still today. In the words of Irish American writer, Frank McCourt,

> If you grew up in Ireland you were told about the Famine. It was dinned into you. In the history books there were pictures of huddled families dying of hunger in their hovels, the same families being evicted—by English landlords—with no place to go but a ditch.

> In the 1930s and 1940s old people in Limerick City still whispered of the horrors of that Famine less than 100 years before. They said it was the fault of the English. They said it was a fact that tons of corn were shipped out of country to feed Her Majesty's armies beyond. There was enough food to go around to feed Ireland ten times over.
>
> The old people said they would never forgive that of the English and they hoped we wouldn't either.[33]

My family was among the Irish Catholics who immigrated to the United States in the nineteenth century during and after the Potato Famine. Many other Irish fled Ireland at this time, and many of them fled to the United States. Ignatiev writes, "From 1815 to the Famine, between 800,000 and one million Irish—about twice the total for the previous two centuries—sailed for North America."[34] And from 1845 to 1855, in a single decade, 1.8 million Irish immigrants came to the United States.[35]

Before the Potato Famine, up to about 1830, most Irish immigrants were from Ulster, and were Presbyterians and Anglicans. According to Ignatiev, these immigrants "did not represent the poorest layers of Irish society; in 1820, American port officials recorded that twenty-seven percent of Irish arriving that year were farmers, twenty-two percent artisans, ten percent tradesmen and professionals, while only twenty-one percent were laborers."[36] However, from the early 1830s, more Catholics than Dissenters and Anglicans began to flee Ireland. As with my family, these famine Irish were consistently Catholic, very poor, and generally from rural areas in Ireland. These immigrants were likely to use Irish, not English, as their first and most important language.[37] In the United States in the mid-nineteenth century, Golway writes that the new immigrants found an "overwhelmingly Protestant country, a place where Catholic churches already had been put to the torch, where the first of many battles already had taken place between immigrant and the native-born. Many more would follow."[38]

When my family came to the United States, they migrated to the west, settling in areas such as "Bloody Kansas," where much of the pre-Civil War violence began. My family came from extreme poverty in Ireland, during and after the Potato Famine. On one side of my family, my mother's mother's father's father, Edward O'Malley, came in 1865. Edward was born in Louisburgh, County Mayo, Ireland, in 1847. This year, known as Black '47, was perhaps the worst in Irish history, and County Mayo was one of the places hardest hit by the Potato Famine. Edward, his two brothers, John and Seamus, and his parents Patrick O'Malley and Honora MacNalley, all five born in Louisburgh, County Mayo, Ireland, eventually moved to Scotland. As an elder cousin of mine succinctly puts it in her version of family history, "due to difficult conditions in Ireland, the family moved to Scotland and settled in Midlem, in Selkirkshire, where three daughters (Bridget, Mary, and Elen) and one more son (Patrick Joseph) were added to the family."[39]

In 1865, the older sons began immigrating to the United States, starting with Edward. After making the long trip across the Atlantic to the Americas, most of my Irish ancestors kept moving. By 1868, Edward, John, and Seamus were all living in Saint Louis, Missouri, with an aunt, Mrs. Martin, and working in the lumber business.

Even though most Irish immigrating to the United States up until the 1830s were not Catholic, there continues to be a popular identification in the United States of "Irish" with "Catholic." My own family puts the two together in naming ourselves. We are Irish Catholic. Yet, the majority of pre-1830s immigrants were Irish Presbyterians who came to be called "Scotch-Irish" or Irish Protestants. They were originally known in the United States as simply "Irish." The common association of Irish with Catholic had to do with a normalizing dualism in which the Scotch-Irish worked to disassociate themselves from the more recent, poorer, and Irish-speaking Catholic immigrants who came to the United States just before and during the Potato Famine. Carl Wittke writes, "The sharp distinction between Irish and Scotch-Irish developed in the United States in the last half of the nineteenth century." As Irish Catholics flooded into the United States during and after the Potato Famine, "the Scotch-Irish insisted upon differentiating between the descendents of earlier immigrants from Ireland," that is, themselves, "and more recent arrivals," the Irish Catholics.[40]

These Irish Catholics who came later were so poor that most could not pay their own ticket for the trip. During the Potato Famine, the only option for many of the destitute Irish Catholics was to die of starvation on the land they farmed (but did not own). Yet, the Irish landlords paid the cost of travel for some as a means to get them off the land.

On another side of my family, my mother's father's mother, Susan Croissen's family went quickly west upon their arrival in the United States. My mother's father's father, Seamus Brennan, came as a teenager, later than many in my family, in 1885. And he too went west. He came with his family to mine coal in Colorado. He and his

one sister lived in Canyon City, Colorado. Seamus moved up in life; that is pretty much the only direction one has to go, coming from the coalmines. Seamus became a superintendent of steam engines in Salida, Colorado. And he married Susan, who turned out to be something close to crazy, perhaps from growing up in poverty and all that poverty brings. Or, of course, there might have been another reason. Or, perhaps, she was simply crazy, the kind of crazy that does not have a reason. It just is.

When the Irish Catholics first arrived in the United States, many lived and worked in and among impoverished and free Black communities. Irish Catholics arrived in the United States as—and understood themselves as—an exploited and oppressed "race," akin to African Americans. Irish Catholics had experienced profound oppression in Ireland, yet not without resistance. They also recognized and resisted the oppressions of others, including that of African Americans in slavery. For example, the Council of Armagh in 1177 banned the Irish from trading in English slaves.[41] Perhaps the most well-known and popular Irish political figure in the first half of the nineteenth century, Daniel O'Connell, when asked to be silent on the issue of slavery replied, "'God knows I speak for the saddest people the sun sees; but may my right hand forget its cunning, and my tongue cleave to the roof of my mouth, if to save Ireland, even Ireland, I forget the negro one single hour!'"[42]

Black and Irish people lived, worked, had children and made families together in neighborhoods such as the Moyamensing district in Philadelphia. The African American and Irish communities also worshipped together. For instance, Ignatiev writes that a church "in Philadelphia was presided over after 1837 by an Afro-American minister; baptismal records for the next twenty years suggest that one-third of the members were Irish."[43]

The Anglo Saxon middle class witnessed Irish and Black intermingling with anxiety and disapproval. A newspaper article described the multiracial inhabitants of a Philadelphia lodging house in horror:

> The walls were discolored by smoke and filth, the glass was broken from the windows, chinks in the frame work let in the cold air, and every thing was as wretchedly uncomfortable as it is possible to conceive. Yet in every one of these squalid apartments, including the cellar and the loft, men and women—blacks and whites by the dozens—were huddled together promiscuously, squatting or lying upon the bare floors, and keeping themselves from freezing by covering their bodies with such filthy rags as chance threw in their way.[44]

While the Irish in the 1800s United States were not Black, they were also not white; so such mixing of communities was not seen by the white middle class to be as terrible as it would have been for Anglo-Saxon and African American people to live and build families together. Although it was ultimately decided that Irish could be naturalized—and many were—their right to citizenship had been disputed due to their unclear "race." About the question of whiteness, Ignatiev writes:

> The first Congress of the United States voted in 1790 that only "white" persons could be naturalized as citizens. Coming as immigrants rather than as captives or hostages undoubtedly affected the potential racial status of the Irish in America, but it did not settle the issue, since it was by no means obvious who was "white." In the early years Irish were frequently referred to as "niggers turned inside out;" the Negroes, for their part, were sometimes called "smoked Irish"[45]

Becoming White

Being Irish could not be the reason for all of the violence, all of the suffering in my family. Everyone seems to have some claim to suffering. But perhaps it is being Irish and Catholic, with our funny mix of being colonized and working hard to move from that position without ever leaving the colonized/colonizer structure behind. And of course, we immigrated in the midst of so much global change, as large parts of the world industrialized. We took part in shaping the United States in the 1800s as industrialization swept across and through the land, a new land for some and an old land for others. In this migration, my Irish ancestors went from a preindustrial society to one rapidly industrializing. Due to the Napoleonic Wars, domestic manufacture increased in the United States. With this expansion in industry came a need for unskilled wage laborers. The new Irish immigrants were among those who filled this need.[46]

The new industrial work that was available tended to involve brutal, unsafe conditions and long hours. The Irish Catholics and others who took up this industrial labor recognized that their lives were in many ways not so different from those who were enslaved. Early on, factory workers often called their work "wage slavery." Nonetheless the Irish moved from being Irish and akin to people of color to being white and understanding themselves as different from, and better than, people of color. As described by historian David R. Roediger, they took the "wages of whiteness" instead of the greater bargaining power of organizing together with all working class people.[47]

Irish Americans are notorious for internalizing a deep and gripping version of western racism. My family was no different. We came out of extreme suffering and went on to impress that suffering on someone else as quickly and as best we could. Indeed when it comes to human beings, it often seems that brutality begets brutality. Instead of continuing to align themselves with the ruthlessly oppressed African Americans after immigrating to the United States, ultimately Irish Catholics reversed their position. Over time, the Irish internalized elite norms and went from being Irish to being normative—to being white. In this, they also began to pride themselves on being not-Black. In the United States, the new Irish Catholic immigrants stepped quickly into the role of the Protestants in Ireland. And like the Protestants in Ireland, Irish Catholic Americans might be living miserable, poverty-stricken lives, yet they could always soothe themselves with their newfound privilege of whiteness.

Because, of course, race is a social construction, not a biological reality, people consciously and unconsciously construct racial groups in a particular society, place, and time. And these constructions change. While the Irish began to understand themselves as being another race and not Black, the work, life, and material conditions of these two groups were not so distinct. Prior to the American Revolution in the eighteenth century, Ignatiev writes, "the range of dependent labor relations had blurred the distinction between freedom and slavery. The Revolution led to the decline of apprenticeship, indenture, and imprisonment for debt."[48] The decline in these slavery-like work relations, along with the growth in slavery itself as the foundation of southern life, "reinforced the tendency to equate freedom with whiteness and slavery with blackness."[49]

After the abolition of slavery, as Roediger points out, past and present-day white working-class people and working-class people of color share many interests economically in the United States.[50] Together they could have organized around their shared power as workers, as "labor." When workers join together, they have the power of their numbers to make demands on those who hire them, the owners/employers or "capital." Coming together as a large group, workers have greater bargaining power, and are in a better position to demand higher wages, shorter working hours, better working conditions, and so on. However, in spite of sharing many concerns, historically white working-class people have organized *against* working-class people of color joining white working-class movements and workplaces, so that the working class in general has been less powerful and more vulnerable.

Why would the white working class harm its own interests by keeping people of color out of white working-class movements? Drawing from the seminal work of the famous African American labor historian W. E. B. Du Bois and his idea about the "psychological wages of whiteness,"[51] Roediger argues that instead of organizing together across racial/ethnic groups to gain greater working class power, "the white working class [settled] for whiteness."[52] In other words, in their racism, the white working class gained something in exchange for their loss of shared working-class power. They settled for the gains of whiteness, or what Roediger, following Du Bois, calls a "psychic wage," that is, "status and privileges conferred by race . . . to make up for the alienating and exploitative class relationships" within which they lived and worked. Roediger writes, "white workers could, and did, define and accept their class positions by fashioning identities as 'not slaves' and as 'not Blacks.'"[53] This is perhaps similar to the situation and choices of Protestant Irish in Ireland. The Protestant Irish, like the white working class in the United States, chose greater psychic power instead of opting for the potential power of greater numbers—bargaining power—had they organized together with the least powerful in their society.

Again drawing from the work of Du Bois, Roediger argues, "White labor does not just receive and resist racist ideas but embraces, adopts and, at times, murderously acts upon those ideas. The problem is not just that the white working class is at critical junctures manipulated into racism, but that it comes to think of itself and its interests as white."[54]

Irish Catholic immigrants like my ancestors took part in a process of normalization whereby they increasingly distanced themselves from African Americans and other working-class people of color. Indeed Roediger argues that "working class formation," the development of an identity as working class, and "the systematic development of a sense of whiteness went hand in hand for the US white working class."[55] As the United States industrialized and a class of people—the working class—developed in and around that industrialization, for those among this group that were white, their new identities as working-class people were inextricably bound with their developing normative identities as white people.[56]

We face my father. As always, we do as he says. We watch. We were in our nightgowns, two small girls, very small. And he took that cat. My sister's cat, all black, soft and sleek, went everywhere with her. Drunk, my father took that cat.

I am a man he told us.

And, he sliced that cat right down the middle.

He gutted my sister's cat. And we watched, late at night, in our nightgowns, in the garage.

Genealogy: My Family Tumbling Through Time

My great grandparents Susan and Seamus had three children, Wilbur, Philip Charles, and a foster daughter, Genevieve. Genevieve married Heyward Bailey and had one daughter, perhaps named after her crazy foster mother, Sue Ann Bailey. Wilbur married Eleanor, became a dentist, and then died young, in his forties. Philip, known as "Cloye," was Susan's most beloved child. Philip, Susan's beloved son, moved from his impoverished coal-mining heritage to medical school and became a doctor, an anesthesiologist. And he married Fiona O'Malley to become, eventually, the parents of my mother.

Like the rest of us, Philip's past gripped him through his life. It gripped him and his children, one of whom is my mother. And it grips me still.

Susan, and her craziness, was the closest thing to a reason for my mother's own story of brutality. Susan offers, like my father's father Clarke, an explanation. The problem is, if you get too close, you find a small Irish girl growing up in dire poverty. Then she ceases to be a reason; she becomes merely another moment in the story's unfolding.

On May 15, 1877, Edward O'Malley from County Mayo married Mary Lyons in Lexington, Missouri. They had seven children including my grandmother Fiona O'Malley's father, Seamus Bernard. Seamus, born in 1879, was the first child. After Seamus came Edward born in 1880, Jerome Grover Cleveland in 1884, Catherine Grace in 1889, John Joseph in 1892, Mary Ruth in 1896, and Peter Samuel in 1899. I grew up visiting two of those children, my great-great-aunts Grace and Ruth, old women, always gentle and kind to me, with odd hairs growing here and there on their faces. Yet, even though Aunt Grace was known to be feisty, even though Aunt Ruth had been a librarian and a spinster and loved to read, we had nothing to say to each other. I remember only a thin connection. Perhaps the connection stayed, always, shallow because my mother left my father, something Catholic women never do. Grace died the year before I finished high school in 1984, and Ruth in 1989, the year I finished college in Colorado Springs, one hour's drive from where she lived in Denver.

I remember sitting with my Gram Brennan, and Aunt Grace and Aunt Ruth on their niece, my grandmother's sister, my great-aunt Elizabeth O'Malley's back patio in an awkward silence. One of my great-aunts told us that it was bad for circulation to sit with your legs crossed. She had read this in a magazine. No one uncrossed her legs. And all of us, with legs crossed, continued to sit in silence.

My grandmother's father, Grace and Ruth's brother, Seamus O'Malley, died in 1912 when my grandmother was not quite seven. She had few memories, but two involved her father. Once, swimming with her, he carried her playfully on his back. And when he died on January 7, 1912, at 33, she was sent by her mother to run for the doctor. She remembered running, running to no avail.

Gram Brennan's mother's father, Keeran, came from County Cork when he was only 13. He was a drummer boy in the Civil War before he married Mary Elizabeth Flood in 1874 in Gentryville, Missouri. Like most Irish Catholics at that time, Keeran stood with—and in his case, drummed for—the Union. After the war, Keeran's wife Mary gave birth to nine children, three of whom died in infancy, and two more as young women. Dying quick and young was what people did in that family. Only four of the nine children survived. My grandmother Brennan's mother, Maime, was one of those four. Maime McKenny married Seamus O'Malley and had two girls, my grandmother Fiona and my great-aunt Elizabeth, before her family's habits rubbed off on Seamus and he died quick and young.

The Judeo-Christian Bible recognizes widows with young children as among the most vulnerable in society. My grandmother Fiona at six, her sister Elizabeth at one, and their widowed mother fit this category. Little Fiona and Elizabeth grew up depending on others. They and their mother Maime lived first with one relative, then with another. Immediately after her husband died, Maime took her two girls and moved in with her brother Frank. When Frank married, Maime had to find another place to stay. Seamus's father Edward had died in 1899. So Maime, a widow, moved in with her husband Seamus's widow mother, Mary Lyons, known, as it turned out unfortunately for Maime, as "Queen Mary." They lived with Mary Lyons in King City, Missouri until Maime finally remarried and moved to Denver, Colorado, with her two children, her new husband, and his children.

The relationship did not last long. And in the end, Maime's younger daughter, Elizabeth, cared for Maime. Elizabeth told me that is what Irish did; they had the youngest daughter live with and care for her elderly parents when and if they reached an age where they needed care. For this, Elizabeth spent her life angry at Fiona. Elizabeth was envious of Fiona for having the life that Elizabeth did not have. Fiona became "lace-curtain Irish" when she married. She married a doctor. She moved up in the world. This was a term the Irish themselves used to describe those Irish who lived in a wealthier part of town, or those like my grandmother Fiona, who owned their houses instead of renting. It was an insult.

If my grandmother, Fiona O'Malley, had lace curtains after she married that was about all she had for Elizabeth to envy. With or without cause, my great aunt Elizabeth envied her sister. She envied her for her husband rather than in spite of him. "Who wanted to marry a woman with an elderly mother to care for?" Elizabeth once asked me angrily. Equally as odd as Elizabeth's anger, Elizabeth's envy, Fiona never seemed to envy Elizabeth, or anyone really. And she had many reasons for envy, many reasons for anger. The man she married, Susan's beloved son Philip known as "Cloye," was brutal as well as drunk, and more brutal when drunk. Philip's mother Susan, who may have been crazy, would regularly and too-often visit her beloved child, Philip, once he was married to Fiona and they had children, Seamus, William, Mary Sue, and Fiona. Fiona, the youngest was my mother and she was unplanned.

My grandmother only told me one thing about Susan and Philip. She told me that one thing when she was in her nineties and we suspected that she had Alzheimer's. We were not sure if it was Alzheimer's or small strokes, perhaps induced by the many beatings she endured. Either way, she seemed to be losing her mind. For some reason, losing her mind meant starting to talk about what had really happened. This was in sharp contrast to her refusal to speak about most things, for most of her life. As though we were meeting at a subdued kind of party, my conversations with my grandmother stayed perpetually stuck in small talk, all my life, all my life until she began to lose her mind. She fasted from speaking for most of her adult life, at least from speaking about her lived experience. And then she became demented and broke her fast. It did not last long before the dementia returned her to a different kind of silence, the silence of a small child, a baby perhaps who is so embedded in the present moment they do not carry all the other moments into this one, right now. At any rate, during the time-of-her-speaking, she told me one thing about Susan and Philip.

We were at her assisted living apartment, waiting for other family members to pick us up and take us to a family gathering. My grandmother's assisted living apartment was also a between-things place, like her speaking during that time. And like the speaking, it did not last long. She moved there with her sister, Elizabeth. They each had their own apartment, only a few floors apart. This was helpful to Elizabeth, who could much more easily control, and resent, her sister if they lived in the same building.

During this brief time between silences and living near her sister, my grandmother told me, her voice filled with disbelief, that whenever her mother-in-law Susan came to visit, she, my grandmother Fiona, would have to move out of the bedroom that she shared with her husband. This was so that he could share the bedroom with his mother. She repeated this to me as though to emphasize how surprising, how unbelievable she found it. And then, our ride came and we left and we never spoke of Susan sleeping with her son, my grandmother's husband Cloye, again.

It is odd that my mother was unplanned. But not because she is Catholic. Catholics do have unplanned children. In a certain sense, that is all they have. For the older generations of Irish Catholics, one has the children one has and one has a lot of them. There is no planning or unplanning to it. Nonetheless, according to my grandmother Fiona, she and her husband only intended to have three children. Given that they were Catholic and thus, supposedly, against birth control, I do not know how they intended this. So the odd thing about my mother being unplanned was that my grandmother and her brutal husband, Philip, ever had intention when it came to children, not that they didn't. Yet, at any rate, this is what my grandmother said. My grandmother told someone this, that they only intended to have three children, in the midst of conversation when my mother was there, an adult woman listening. My mother, surprised, said to her mother, but you had four? And her mother, my grandmother, also surprised, found herself caught in a disclosure, much like having her fourth child, my mother, a disclosure that she had not intended.

Does my mother's unplanned status make me unplanned too, and my sister and my brother? Are my children also accidents that happened, springing forth from a tiny moment, a happening outside of mindfulness, outside of intention, that became my mother? Are we all merely a bursting forth of fate, one event bumping and falling into another, and another?

Before my mother was a grown woman and discovered she was unplanned, when she was still a little girl, her grandmother Susan would come and visit her family in their home in Denver, Colorado. And when she came, Philip, like his mother, fell into craziness. He drank more and more. And he became more and more brutal. I do not fully understand what happened between him and his mother that led to this reaction. Supposedly Susan loved Philip; she loved him immensely, intensely, too much. But how could love, with its deep desire for the well-being of the beloved, bring about such a whirlwind of bashing, drunken, out-of-controlness. Whatever she felt for Philip, he went crazy during and after his mother's visits. Thus, not only were Susan's visits too frequent, but inevitably her visits went on too long, and always longer than originally planned.

Once early on in her marriage to Philip, when Fiona just had the one small child, her oldest Seamus, after a particularly bad beating, she took her baby and fled. She returned home to her mother and her envious sister, Elizabeth. As far as I know, this was the only time she fought back. Leaving, like many things that appear otherwise, can be a way of fighting, fighting hard. She did what Irish Catholic women do not do, she left her husband. Her mother and Elizabeth let her stay the one night. And then, and then, they sent her back. As far as I know, she never, ever left again.

Along with alcohol, Philip seemed to be addicted to gambling. Even the house, with lace curtains, was a product of Philip's addictions. He won the house that he, Fiona, and their four children lived in for their whole life as a family. When Philip died suddenly of cancer in his early sixties, the children were all grown, the youngest, my mother, having just finished her first year of college, but Fiona and Philip were still in that house. And while Fiona went to work as a social worker, because Philip had gambled everything away and left her with nothing but the house, she continued to live in that lace-curtain house he had won.

Somehow, in the midst of being tossed from home to home as a child, and regularly facing violence as an adult, my Gram, Fiona Brennan, went on living. And throughout the ordeal of it all, she had the consistency of her religion. She was, of course, Irish Catholic. Indeed the religiosity of the women in my family remains consistent through our story. Even my mother, even me, we weave religion into the daily fabric of our lives.

And so it makes sense that religion frames most of my childhood memories. Even the last memory I have of Ruth O'Malley involves our love of it. In the memory, my grandmother drives me to visit Aunt Ruth, then 93 years old. She was not home in her little Denver, Colorado, apartment. I could feel as we entered the stillness that my grandmother held her breath. We both wondered if the quiet spoke loudly of Aunt Ruth's death. Yet quickly my grandmother could see that Aunt Ruth had taken her going-out-things and gone out. So my grandmother and I, knowing where Aunt Ruth would be, drove Aunt Ruth's short walk to church and found her, nearly blind and fully resolute, making her daily pilgrimage to mass.

My Grandfather-Who-Did-Not-Want-To-Be-Called-Grandfather

It is odd that I know so little about him. He was Aldous Clarke before he became my grandfather-who-did-not-want-to-be-called-grandfather, and so we called him Clarke. And like my mother's father, my father's father was also brutal. But unlike crazy, drunk Philip, the son of crazy Susan, Clarke's brutality was sane, measured, under control. Perhaps this was because he was Protestant. Clarke got rich in the cattle business. My grandmother, his wife Jean, told me that his family was proslavery. One imagines that this and being Protestant would have been enough to turn my grandmother, Jean Halley's family against him. Yet my grandmother's mother, May, had beat Jean to the punch and already done the same thing, herself. Her transgression must have tempered the family's response to Jean's.

My grandmother Jean Halley's father, Tulesis Cisero Halley, who was named by his only sister, Georgia, started a sheep ranch near Carr, Colorado. He was a sheep man. Along with being a rancher and farmer, Tull was a Baptist. This was enough for my Gram's mother's mother to be against her daughter May marrying Tull. Irish Catholics were understood to be another race, distinct from the Anglo-Saxon white community, distinct and fundamentally lower, less civilized, less trustworthy, less capable, less intelligent. The only thing Irish Catholics were thought to do more of was drink alcohol and have babies. Irish Catholics often responded to this prejudice by sticking with their own. This is to say that it would have been a scandal for both sides that she married a Protestant and he married a Catholic. For her side, she did gain the concession that the children would be raised Catholic. And they were.

One supposes that perhaps May felt the same way when it was no longer her but her elegant daughter, Jean, marrying a Protestant cattleman whose family was proslavery. Further, back then in the West, sheepherders, like Jean's father, Tull, and cattle ranchers were deeply antagonistic. So this antagonism must have added an extra punch to Jean's decision. Yet I was told no stories of upset on either side of the family.

Oddly repetitive in their life stories, May and her daughter Jean had also both been engaged to be married to other men prior to their actual weddings, weddings to those who became my family. May's fiancé died suddenly of pneumonia and Jean's first engagement was, for reasons I do not know, broken off. So May married Protestant Tull and they became my grandmother's parents. And later Jean married Aldous soon to become the parents of my father, Simon. Protestant men did nothing to stop Catholicism from pouring into our family's future. May raised her children Catholic. And Jean's five children, all boys, were also all raised Catholic.

And that led to my mother Fiona and my father, my father who was drunk in the garage, meeting. Because Kidron, Wyoming, where Aldous and Jean raised their five boys, did not have a good Catholic high school, or even a bad one, they sent their eldest son Simon to Denver to go to Regis High School, the Catholic boy's school. My mother Fiona went to the "sister" Catholic girl's school. And she met

Simon. And she agreed to marry although she did not want to. She did not want to marry Simon or marry at all. Yet she was Catholic and Catholic girls get married. And anyhow, when she finally told Simon that she did not want to marry him, he reminded her that the wedding invitations were already printed. It was too late to back out now. So they married and moved to Grand Junction, Wyoming, where they bought a house with a two-car garage, a garage with a cold cement floor. And my mother was caught.

She came from brutality and married it. Like all of us tumbling through time, in motion, and held tightly, all at once.

Maybe it was the alcohol. Maybe not. But something, something blurred the lines around reality. Nothing was clear. And now, looking back, I still wonder. Am I remembering this right? Is this really it? I did not know then, so how can I possibly be sure now.

And My Gram

Who was this woman, my grandmother? If I knew, would her story set me free? If I knew, would knowing take this weight away, this forever pain? Or is it, simply, too late? Always, too late.

And, anyhow, maybe my grandmother told me all I need to know. My grandmother chose not to want the truth. She chose to look the other way. And oddly, this is the thing I despise most in everyone else, everyone except my grandmother. I don't know why, but I can, I do forgive my grandmother. And my grandmother chose this thing. She chose not to see. And in a way, she told me this. She told me of her choice.

Let me tell you a memory I never had to remember. It was one of those always-there memories. Somehow this memory got mixed in with all the regular memories, the memories that I did not have to forget. It was a memory that crossed over, leading me, taking me away from my family's story, our established family story, the story we lived in. It is a memory of shame.

In this memory, I am sitting on Clarke's lap. I am eight or so. Too big to be pulled into a grown man's lap, even if he is my grandfather. In the memory, Clarke has his hand in my shirt, and he is touching my absolutely flat child chest. I can tell you now that I did not like this. And, I can tell you that I did not understand. Yet there is no point in telling you because it simply did not matter. Clarke is Clarke. He does whatever he wants and no one asks questions. There is no room for saying no. And certainly no room for the voice of an eight-year-old girl. If anyone is no one, it is I. Well, in the memory, Gram walks in. We are in Clarke's den, sitting on Clarke's couch. Clarke has his television here, in the den, and a big window that looks down over the rose garden, the rose garden that I love. Gram walks in, she walks into Clarke's den to call us to supper. She walks in, and she sees what is happening. There are so many things I would like to be able to tell you now, so many things. But it is too late for me, too late for lying. So I will tell you what Gram did. She walked in and saw what was happening. And then, she turned around and walked out.

Chapter 4

The Production of Animal Life: The Early American Cattle Business

In this chapter, I describe the lives of and the business surrounding cows in the early years of the nation, including the role that cows played in colonization. I also examine the growing function of American corn, the plant one might argue that has colonized us all. Along with corn's impact, I explore shifting notions of time from what historian E. P. Thompson calls "natural" time to the clock time that came with industrialization. Finally, I investigate the journey of cows at the end of their lives when they travel to slaughterhouses to be transformed into meat. Here we see an early biopolitical way of thinking about cows, as colonists began to control and attempt to enhance animal life, to make more cow, more meat, and eventually, more money, in less and less time. Both Thompson and Foucault illuminate how transforming the ways humans relate to time, enhanced human and cow capacity to produce more (not only meat but most things), more quickly.

Early American cows lived a vastly different life than contemporary meat industry cattle. In the very beginning, colonists let them run wild and simply captured and killed them for food when food was needed or desired. Over time, herders began to organize their herds, having some sense of who and where the cows were, and gathering them regularly for slaughter and the making of meat.

In the twentieth century, cows became a central part of the US diet. Yet common US meals did not always include beef. From colonization until the 1870s, pork was the primary meat eaten in the United States. The English colonizers brought this habit with them from England. Anthropologist Eric B. Ross observes, "By the time that English settlers began to colonize the eastern seaboard of North

America, it was widely recognized in the Old World that 'no animal was so easily fed, and no animal so easily put on flesh' as the hog."[1] Until 1850, Ross notes that following wheat, Americans ate more pig than any other "'article of provisions.'"[2] Indeed, Ross continues, "Until quite recently in the United States . . . , pork usually was consumed at a rate equal to or greater than beef."[3] Pigs were easy to feed, and adapted readily to and rapidly put on weight in their new environment. "Especially with Indian corn to supplement nuts and other forage, pigs quickly achieved a strategic edge and pork a place in the diet which cattle and beef could not rival."[4]

Nonetheless, while pigs were merely eaten, cattle played a variety of roles in colonial human lives. Ross writes, "Cattle, more than swine, may have represented wealth, their ownership being in general a function of capital resources." Along with meat, cows were important because of the milk, butter, and hide that they supplied, and as draft (work) animals. Indeed, the value of cows lay less in their capacity to produce meat than in dairy products, and in their strength and ability to work.[5]

The importance of pigs as food stemmed from the fact that their meat could be effectively and tastily preserved. Without railroads or refrigeration, fresh meat tended to be slaughtered locally and eaten quickly. Prerefrigeration pork, however, could be preserved relatively easily, safely, and with significantly better flavor than beef. Ross writes that given the "methods of preservation up to the 1870s—curing, pickling, salting—processed pork was more flavorsome than beef and was often to be trusted, especially in warmer regions, where fresh meat was not." The preserved meat of pigs could be transported more easily than the live animals. Interestingly, in contrast to cows, live pigs were more difficult to move from place to place. As living animals, pigs were "harder to drive, had a higher mortality rate and were more susceptible to shrinkage in transit."[6]

Albeit not eaten at the same rate as pigs, cows were food as well as valuable domestic work animals in colonial and postcolonial communities. As these communities grew and land filled up, cattle herders routinely moved further west, pushing the frontier as they went, further and further west too. Along with organizing, and in some sense, knowing their cows, herders also began to actively care for them. Caring included fencing them in. Colonial Maryland was one of the last to take up this change as it meant that actual labor was expended in exchange for the domestic meat gained. The winter of 1694–1695 presented a challenge to the relaxed approach when 25,000 cows and 60,000 pigs died due to the harsh weather.[7] After that, even

Maryland began to care for its cattle, offering them food and shelter during the winter months.

In contrast to Maryland, herders in Pennsylvania cared for their cows from early on. In fact, of all the colonies, Pennsylvania took the best care of their cattle. In Pennsylvania, Skaggs writes that even on the "frontier it was unusual for colonists' animals to be untended, turned loose to forage in the wild woods."[8] Because they paid attention, they noticed what was good food, and what was bad, for cows. For example, for their dairy cows, they found red clover to be instrumental in producing sweet milk and cheese.

As herders pushed their cattle west, they themselves were pushed west by the white "civilization" expanding behind them. Settlers followed herders. They cleared the land of woods and began to plow it. Farmland left little room for cows to forage, so the herders moved again. And then they moved again, and then again.

As the result of their movement, in the late 1600s, the herders founded what was to be, according to Skaggs, the "first great cow country of American history" in the foothills of the Appalachian Mountains. It was a cow's Eden. "Animals ran free, grazing on luxuriant river-bottom grasses and on tangled peavines that choked hillsides."[9] Yet, even in Eden, cows can expect an unnatural death. When the time came to cash in on the cows, herders captured these essentially wild animals by chasing them—both cow and human on foot—into a river's fork. The fork acted like a corral. After gathering the cows, the herders and their dogs drove them into forest clearings. These areas were cleared of trees in the midst of Appalachian forest and they acted much like future cowpens. Temporary towns sprung up around the forest clearings. These frontier towns were similar to the Dodge City of two hundred years later. "Animals collected in the cowpens were eventually driven eastward in herds of several hundred head to markets at Charleston, Baltimore and even Philadelphia."[10]

Over time the early cattle business grew. The material conditions in the United States, a relatively young country possessing large areas of grassland inhabited by relatively few humans, allowed for beef production and the growth of the cattle business. Ross writes, "The principle beef-producing and beef-consuming areas of the world ... are in countries that possess considerable and sparsely inhabited grassland—characteristics, in general, of comparatively young countries." Ross continues, "With increasing population and accompanying rises in land values, extensive forms of production such as cattle grazing tend to yield to more intensive forms of agriculture—usually based on cereals—and more efficient forms of protein production such as raising swine or dairy cows."[11]

The early US cattle business faced many obstacles, but grew in spite of them. During the Revolutionary War, meat sold poorly from the United States to other places because the British controlled much of the seas. In fact, the West Indian meat and cattle trade stopped completely during the war. Battles themselves halted the meat business in the areas right around the fight. Yet overall, even in this time of war, cow herders flourished, Skaggs writes, "because of the inordinate demand of British armies in North America, which paid pounds in sterling."[12]

Following the Revolutionary War, people in the cattle business became more serious about the care of their cattle. In 1791 in Maine, Charles and Benjamin Vaughan even made an effort to improve the cows themselves through conscious breeding. They brought a special Bakewell bull from England and infused his blood into their Maine cows. If it were not for Maine's harsh winters, the Vaughans and others in Maine might have developed a prospering cattle industry much like that in the Carolinas. Maine was open and uncrowded, offering cows lots of space to roam. But Maine's winters were very harsh, too harsh for raising cows. And albeit cold, which is good for processing meat, Maine was too far away from everything, and too underpopulated, to be good for killing cows.[13]

Instead, cows were raised along the ever-moving western frontier. At the end of their days, they were herded back east to places, such as the land in upstate New York, and that surrounding Philadelphia, where they were fattened up for slaughter. These animals were then sent to be killed by meatpackers in Philadelphia and Manhattan.

During the 1700s, science entered the realm of animal husbandry. In fact, the United States holds the dubious honor of being the place where scientific husbandry originated—dubious because science has not meant better lives for cows nor, perhaps, for the people raising, slaughtering, and eating them either. Modern science with its partner, industrialization, has meant starkly different lives for farm animals—shorter lives, lives lived in greater sickness, smaller spaces, and with less, if any, sunshine, lives often ending in more painful deaths. Scientific husbandry also accompanied the beginning of biopolitics, that is the beginning of a focused, organized effort to manipulate, enhance (in the sense of making more cow, faster), and control cow life.

About animal husbandry, Skaggs writes, "In 1749, Benjamin Franklin had called on colonial colleges to teach agriculture as a regular part of their curricula, and fifteen years later he participated in the founding of the Philadelphia Society for Promoting Agriculture."[14] The Massachusetts State Agricultural Society was founded in 1792.

In 1793, Waltham, Massachusetts, put on one of the first agricultural fairs. And in the next several decades, more and more communities sponsored similar agricultural groups, exhibitions, and fairs. All were interested in championing improved—scientific—agricultural methods. One method of "improvement" entailed introducing and developing new breeds of cattle.

These agricultural techniques spread through the new agricultural press that emerged in the early 1800s with the *Agricultural Museum* founded in 1810 in Washington, DC. The *American Farmer* started in 1819. Considered to be one of the best agricultural publications, it was one of the longest lasting as well. From 1810 to the beginning of the Civil War in the United States, 250 new agricultural publications came out. Along with articles about the enhancing of livestock, these publications discussed the production records and weight of prize stock and the differences between breeds.[15]

Since colonial times, raising and caring for cows was financially viable only if land was cheap or if the animals could forage for free. Around the turn of the century, around 1800, the frontier with its promise of cheap, "wild" land had moved over the Appalachian Mountains to the Ohio Valley. Skaggs notes, "After the native Indian population was removed by the Treaty of Greenville (1795), the whole Ohio country was thrown open to white immigration. During the last five years of the eighteenth century, 20,000 [non-Native] Americans crossed the mountains into the new West."[16] In other words, conquest and cows opened US land for white immigrants as they pushed their frontier west and west again. Cows also played a central role in displacing the indigenous people living west of the moving white frontier. Cattle signaled that more land was about to be usurped and cattle devoured the land's offerings until white and other farmers came along and moved the cattle further west again. Thus in the early 1800s, well before the Civil War, the Ohio Valley—present-day central Kentucky—became the heart of the US livestock business.

The Ohio Valley had rich soil and a growing season that was perfect for corn. Now it should be said that corn is a flexible plant. This very flexibility helps account for its great success on a global scale today. Corn fairly happily adjusts to a lot of diverse environments, making itself at home in many different places. Yet corn grew especially well in the Ohio Valley. Around 1800, there was already a surplus of corn on the market. This surplus has grown to the enormous glut of corn on our markets today. Because of the surplus, it made economic sense to feed corn to cows rather than dispose of it on the market where there was already too much supply. In 1824, corn was selling for only ten cents a bushel. So the solution, "the only solution" writes historian Paul C. Henlein, was to "convert the corn into marketable produce—whisky, fat cattle, and fat hogs."[17] Whereas this did make economic sense, it made no sense in terms of cows. Cows are animals that evolved to eat grass rather than grain. But this was business, and business often trumps evolution in US history. What is evolution in the face of a profit?

A Brief History of Corn

Here again we see the biopolitical management of life, in this case, plant life. As discussed in journalist Michael Pollan's impressive book, *The Omnivore's Dilemma: A Natural History of Four Meals*, corn is at the root (so to speak) of nearly all of our food in the United States today, at least our food if one eats—as most of us do—at the industrial food chain's table. Pollan writes, "The great edifice of variety and choice that is an American supermarket turns out to rest on a remarkably narrow biological foundation comprised of a tiny group of plants that is dominated by a single species: Zea mays, the giant tropical grass most Americans know as corn."[18] It is not simply a matter of us eating a lot of corn, that is, *as corn*. An American can go a whole year eating no actual corn—golden kernels, on or off the cob—and nonetheless be eating mostly corn. This is because most of the meat produced in the United States eats corn, that is, when it is still a living being. And corn makes up much of our processed foods too. Using modified cornstarch, corn flour, corn oil, and corn syrup, we create our many highly processed foods.[19] In fact, corn is not just what we eat, it is a component of *where* we eat. Corn serves as an important part of the environment from which we purchase, cook, and serve our food. "Indeed, the supermarket itself—the wallboard and joint compound, the linoleum and fiberglass and adhesives out of which the building itself has been built—is in no small measure a manifestation of corn."[20] As Pollan reveals, we feed our domestic animals corn. Those destined to be meat—including fish such as the catfish, tilapia, and salmon—and those that produce eggs and milk, all eat corn. Corn upon corn upon corn. We eat corn. How this happened; how we happened to become so focused on one food, one grain, corn, is an interesting story in itself. This story is important because it reveals how both cow and human lives are manipulated in the interest of (bio)capital.

Pollan argues that corn colonized us, our land, our bodies. And if we really *are* what we eat—and much of science shows that, indeed, we are—then *we* are corn. Corn came to us from southern Mexico where people like the Mayans ate corn as a staple for thousands of years.[21] From southern Mexico, corn traveled north and beat Europeans to North America by four or five hundred years. Scholars argue that Native North Americans have been cultivating corn since around 1000 BCE (Before the Common Era). As corn moved, it adapted quickly to the new environments that it faced. One of the reasons corn has done so well—if by doing well one means existing, and being consumed in abundance—is that its "genetic variability allows it to adapt rapidly to new conditions." Pollan writes that corn has "made itself at home in virtually every microclimate in North America; hot or cold, dry or wet, sandy soil or heavy, short day or long, corn, with the help of its Native American allies, evolved whatever traits it needed to survive and flourish."[22]

Even today people in Central America and Mexico eat a lot of corn, and the Mayans "still sometimes refer to themselves as 'the corn people' … Forty percent of the calories a Mexican eats in a day comes directly from corn, most of it in the form of tortillas. So when a Mexican says 'I am maize' or 'corn walking,' it is simply a statement of fact: The very substance of the Mexican's body is to a considerable extent a manifestation of this plant."[23] We too, in the United States are made of corn, except in our case it is highly processed corn.

Scientists can see the corn in us, by studying what are called isotope ratios in our bodies. Pollan writes: "Researchers who have compared the isotopes in the flesh or hair of North Americans to those in the same tissues of Mexicans report that it is now we in the North who are the true people of corn. 'When you look at the isotope ratios,' [claimed] Todd Dawson, a Berkeley biologist … 'we North Americans look like corn chips with legs.'"[24]

Native people taught the Pilgrims how to plant and grow corn only shortly after the arrival of the first cows to the area, in 1621. The Pilgrims were wheat-eaters, and whereas corn did not make the breads they were used to, it did offer an immense versatility. The Pilgrims ate corn fresh off of the cob. They dried it on the stalk and stored it for months. They ground it into flour. They used corn to make their alcohol, including both corn beer and corn whiskey. They made rugs and twine from corn husks. Their livestock ate the leaves and stalks as fodder. Further, the Pilgrims both burned the shelled cobs for heat and used them for toilet "paper."[25] It is hard to imagine a more useful or well-used plant.

It is fascinating that corn evolved to need us as much, if not more, than we need it. The plant needs an animal to remove its husk—a process that demands an opposable thumb—take the seeds off and plant them in the ground. If a whole cob of corn is planted, the husk either smothers the kernels or if they get free, they are too close together and crowded to be able to survive as they each grow into a plant with leaves. No wild corn exists. The domestic plant is thought to have come from teosinte, a weedy grass that does not look like corn at all. Pollan explain, "The current thinking among botanists is that several thousand years ago teosinte underwent an abrupt series of mutations that turned it into corn; geneticists calculate that changes on as few as four chromosomes could account for the main traits that distinguish teosinte from maize."[26] These mutations meant that corn "lost its ability to reproduce itself." This, of course, is no small loss.

> A mutation this freakish and maladaptive would have swiftly brought the plant to an evolutionary dead end had one of those freaks not happened to catch the eye of a human somewhere in Central America who, looking for something to eat, peeled open the husk to free the seeds. What would have been an unheralded botanical catastrophe in a world without humans became an incalculable evolutionary boon. If you look hard enough, you can still find teosinte growing in certain Central American highlands; you can find maize, its mutant offspring, anywhere you find people.[27]

Over time farmers became more and more adept at growing more and more corn with less and less labor. And the farmers, and the corn—as is so often the case with big business in the United States—had the help of the federal government. The government intervened in corn's story in a number of ways. Most importantly, soon after World War II, the government gifted corn with chemical fertilizer. Pollan writes, "After the war the government had found itself with a tremendous surplus of ammonium nitrate, the principle ingredient in the making of explosives."[28] The federal government busied itself with turning the war economy into a peacetime economy and this meant using all the leftover stuff of war for the business of life-without-war. In this effort, the federal government reinvented ammonium nitrate as a fertilizer. It turned out ammonium nitrate not only makes great killing mechanisms, it also makes great food for plants. And so our plants devoured the leftover ingredients of the war. And we too ate well of war, as we ate the plants that ate the ammonium nitrate, and the animals that ate the plants that ate the ammonium nitrate. We all dined richly.

A Brief History of Time: Time Changes

Well before we began to dine on ammonium nitrate, many of us humans also began to consume time. In exploring the origins of

Irish Americans, but even more starkly in looking at the origins of US cows, one cannot help but explore the changes in our normative sense of time. These time changes coincided with the process of industrialization. Cows probably cannot tell time; nonetheless, they offer a quintessential example of the changes in time sense and the changes' effects on everyday life. Cows' very bodies enacted the social movement from a preindustrial to an industrialized world where time held value.

US cows used to live longer lives, have smaller bodies, roam larger spaces, and consume more food that cows evolved to eat, that is, grass. Cows had cow-lives closer to the lives cows evolved to live when left to their own devices. And, their people lived more present-oriented lives. People focused more on, and centered life around, the present moment.

In his brilliant essay, "Time, Work-Discipline, and Industrial Capitalism," Thompson writes about the normalizing shift from such present-oriented understandings of time to our contemporary clock time, a conception of time, I argue, that focuses always on the future. Thompson points to the depth of this change—from an understanding of time as "natural" to time bound by the clock—in the culture of Western Europe. About cultures centered on "nature's" time, Thompson claims, "It is well known that among primitive [*sic*] peoples the measurement of time is commonly related to familiar processes in the cycle of work or of domestic chores."[29] By way of example, he continues, "labour from dawn to dusk can appear to be 'natural' in a farming community, especially in the harvest months: nature demands that the grain be harvested before the thunderstorms set in. And we may note similar 'natural' work-rhythms which attend to other rural or industrial occupations; sheep must be attended at lambing time and guarded from predators; cows must be milked."[30] Thompson avoids romanticizing such "natural" time orientations. Life could be brutal in preindustrial Western Europe, for example, where the vast majority of people struggled to survive as peasant farmers.

With the industrial revolution, the sense of time based on the rhythms of work and bodies, seasons and the sun, shifted to an understanding of time bound to clocks. In an industrialized world, one gets up and goes to work in a factory at the same clock time each day whether, or not, the sun has come up. In winter the days are shorter, and in summer they are longer, yet with the industrial revolution, work does not begin each day at the same natural time (when the sun rises). Rather, the day begins at the same *clock time*—perhaps 9 a.m.—with or without daylight.

Thompson argues against technological determinism; the clock did not make this shift in understandings of time happen. Rather, a fundamental change in human culture brought about an excess of clocks. About this change in "time-sense," Thompson writes, "As the seventeenth century moves on, the image of clock-work extends, until, with Newton, it has engrossed the universe. And by the middle of the eighteenth century ... the clock had penetrated to more intimate levels."[31]

Thompson explores the depth of the clock's penetration, investigating our work, our working habits, and our very sense of selfhood. He asks,

> How far, and in what ways, did this shift in time-sense affect labour discipline, and how far did it influence the inward apprehension of time of working people? If the transition to mature industrial society entailed a severe restructuring of working habits—new disciplines, new incentives, and a new human nature upon which these incentives could bite effectively—how far is this related to changes in the inward notation of time?[32]

In answering these questions, Thompson shows that at least those in the middle class in industrialized nations, have internalized clock time in a manner so fundamental, so deep-seated that we assume it to be natural, more natural than nature. Clock time has become normative. In this internalization, we embody a "restless urgency ... [a] desire to consume time purposively."[33] And we shake our heads in disgust at those from other cultures who fail "to respond to incentives and disciplines"[34] much like author John Foster, in 1821, upon discovering that:

> A considerable proportion of manual workers ... after concluding their work were left with 'several hours in the day to be spent nearly as they please. And in what manner ... is this precious time expended by those of no mental cultivation ... We shall often see them just simply annihilating those portions of time. They will for an hour, or hours together ... sit on a bench, or lie down on a bank or hillock ... yielded up to utter vacancy and torpor.'[35]

Foucault also addresses time and our shift in time sense. He posits two new ways of thinking about time that came about; one, a negative way, "the principle of non-idleness." Here Foucault writes that in this framework, it was often "forbidden to waste time, which was counted by God and paid for by men." And two, Foucault argues that we also developed a positive principle "of a theoretically ever-growing use of time." Foucault notes that in this we work to extract "from time, ever more available moments and, from each moment ever more useful forces. This means that one must seek to intensify the use of the slightest moment, as if time, in its very fragmentation, were inexhaustible." In part, normalization developed through these new ways of thinking about time.[36]

My great-aunt Elizabeth was attached, both, to time and to anger. And she used her time well to satisfy her determination to be angry. Time's passing afforded her many gratifying opportunities. My grandmother, her older sister Fiona, filled in as the object toward whom Elizabeth directed her anger. She managed to find cause for anger at Fiona whenever possible, and when no cause presented itself, she assembled one. Elizabeth hated lateness. My grandmother hated neither lateness nor earliness, nor much of anything else. My grandmother tended to be on time. Elizabeth, determined to be angry, made my grandmother late for their many appointments by turning up early herself. That way, when she picked up my grandmother to go somewhere, she could stand outside her car, arms crossed, neck tensed, furious at my grandmother for making her wait the span of time from when she showed up early to when they had arranged to meet.

Thompson acknowledges that there is no way to know for certain if, or how much, everyone in any modern industrialized nation such as the United States is gripped by clock time. However, he writes, "it is possible to offer one check of a comparative kind. For what was said by the mercantilist moralists as to the failures of the eighteenth-century English poor to respond to incentives and disciplines is often repeated, by observers and by theorists of economic growth, of the peoples of developing countries today. Thus Mexican paeons in the early years of this century were regarded as an 'indolent and childlike people.'"[37]

Perhaps my great-aunt Elizabeth felt this way about my grandmother.

Cows Save Time: Growing Fat *Fast* on Corn

In contrast to valuing time, in contrast to eating corn, cattle evolved to eat grass, and to take their time about it. They perform a kind of magic in their ability to digest, fatten, and thrive on this particular plant. Cows have an organ called a rumen that breaks down the cellulose in grass allowing cows access to the nutrients. The grass makes use of the sun's energy and offers its nutrients to rumens. When managed properly, the rumens will eat just the right amount of grass, in just the right amount of bites, to actually aid the grass in growing back strong and healthy again and again. The rumens help to grow new grass. Pollan explains:

> Not only do ruminants spread and fertilize seed with their manure, but their hoofprints create shady little pockets of exposed soil where water collects—ideal conditions for germinating a grass seed. And in brittle lands during the driest summer months, when microbial life in the soil all but stops, the rumen of the animals takes over the soil's nutrient-cycling role, breaking down dry plant matter into basic nutrients and organic matter, which the animals then spread in their urine and manure.[38]

Human omnivores can eat a lot of things, but without a rumen, grass is not one of them.

Nonetheless, in spite of being grass-eaters by nature, our ancestral cows ate corn, and our contemporary cows still eat corn, tons and tons of corn. In managing cow life, humans found that cows eating corn means more cow, faster. Plus, we had a lot of corn, and the market demanded that we do something with it. So, cows have been eating corn for a couple hundred years in the United States. Ross notes, "By 1912, 74% of the total feed costs of beef cattle were represented by corn."[39] However, they also ate lots of grass, along with corn, back in the Ohio Valley.

In fact, in the Ohio Valley, in the early 1800s, cows ate bluegrass. Henlein explains, "Bluegrass pasture became one leg, and corn the other, upon which the cattle industry of central Kentucky stood." The cattle ranchers "wintered their two-year-olds out of doors on shocked [*sic*] corn, put them on bluegrass in the spring and summer, and then stuffed them with corn until February, when the drive to market began."[40]

Pigs that fed on the undigested corn in the cattle manure often accompanied the cattle drives. Cow systems manage on corn, yet eating it does not allow for the fine-tuned dance that evolved between cows and grass. Some of the corn just goes right through their system. Pigs, being pigs, offered the corn a second chance at producing profit. They helped the ranchers get the most out of their corn.

To get the most out of bluegrass, cattle ranchers began to open up the woodland and turn it into bluegrass pasture. Bluegrass offers us another migration story. Bluegrass was not originally from Kentucky but Virginia. Henlein writes, "In 1792 Thomas Goff made a trip back to Virginia to fetch a wife; while on this trip, says one local Kentucky story, he saw his horse eating a strange grass (bluegrass) in the Powell Valley and brought some seed back with him to Kentucky." Henlein found that bluegrass was not common in North America. Edward N. Wentworth wrote to Henlein, "I have always heard that it reached Virginia by chance as some extra feed for livestock, presumably horses, which were imported there." So it turns out that many of us are not from here, not even cows, not even Kentucky bluegrass, and certainly not my Irish American family who did not arrive in the Americas until decades after bluegrass made its way to Kentucky.[41]

In Kentucky, cattle ranchers found that cattle grew fat on bluegrass, and particularly on bluegrass growing in pastures cleared of trees. Bluegrass grows in woodlands, but it grows best on forest-free land, and it turns out, so do cows. On May 24, 1856, a cattle rancher wrote in the Ohio Farmer, "Woodland pastures will keep young stock growing, and old ones on foot, but will not fatten them. A three-year-old Durham, or a five-year-old Patton, and common ox, will get 'stall-fat' in a year on open blue grass."[42] So woodlands were cleared for cattle, for bluegrass and for corn.

As time passed, a smaller and smaller group of companies and men made more and more of the money to be made off of meat. There were, and are, plenty of ups and downs in the cattle business. Yet sometimes it seems that the business has been more about downs than ups, especially for the cows, but for the ranchers as well. For example, Skaggs relates that because of a drought in 1837, cattle ranchers dumped their cows on "an already depressed market for whatever prices they would bring."[43] Later in 1843 and 1845 to 1849, bountiful corn crops were a reason for ranchers to raise more cattle. With this cow population growth, more cows were slaughtered and thus the price of beef went down again.

From the Civil War to World War I, industrialization and new and rapidly developing technology changed meatpacking from a "localized, seasonal endeavor of a couple hundred small businessmen into a year-round, fast paced, nationally integrated commodity supply system dominated by five giant companies commonly called the 'beef trust.'"[44] Upton Sinclair wrote his famous book, *The Jungle*, about this system.[45] It was not only enormous in size, but enormously powerful. Skaggs writes:

> In 1850, 185 establishments nationwide prepared $12 million worth of red meat; in 1919, 1,304 plants produced $4.2 billion worth,

measured in dollars that had appreciated in value by one-third. By then American meatpacking was among the nation's largest contributors to the gross national product, only recently having been surpassed by the automobile industry as America's largest employer.[46]

The Line Production System

There exists another interesting link between meatpacking and the automobile industry, between cows and cars. Henry Ford first used the line production system in his Highland Park, Michigan, automobile factory. This system made industrial production produce more cars while costing Ford less.[47] Based on the scientific management production process invented by Frederick Taylor, the line production system broke down the work required to make a car—or slaughter an animal and pack its flesh—into tiny steps adding up to the complete task. Instead of one person slaughtering and packing one whole cow from start to finish, each worker began to do only one tiny piece of that whole. Coinciding with this change, workers went from being skilled (butchers) to unskilled.[48] Not only was the work done more quickly, but any given worker was less valuable. Each worker was easy to train and easily replaceable, and so could be paid less. About this transformation in work, historian Stuart Ewen writes:

> For the workers, the movement toward mass production had severely changed the character of labor. The worker had a decreasingly "significant" unit of production within the modern manufacturing process. "The man who had been the more or less creative maker of the whole of an article became the tender of a machine that made only one small part of the article." The time required to teach the worker the "adept performance" of his "operation on assembly work" was a matter of a few hours.[49]

As Thompson explains, time had become money.[50] The slaughterhouse goal entailed producing as much meat as possible with the least expense in as little time as possible. Time itself mattered.

Industrialization and Biopolitical Cows: Bovines in Motion through (Clock) Time

With the prices up or down, people were not after cows, but beef. To fulfill this desire, the cattle had to go through a transformation from cow to meat. And live cow or dead meat, the flesh had to be transported to the markets where meat was sold. Early on in the beef industry, cows carried their own meat all the way from wherever they were fattened to the market. As mentioned previously, although pigs remained the primary meat on US tables until at least 1850, pigs have never traveled as well as cows. In the first half of the nineteenth century, Ohio Valley cattle walked east across the mountains to be remade into meat for city markets. And over time the numbers of cattle ballooned. Skaggs notes that 700 cows walked to their deaths in 1810, "1,500 in 1815, 7,000 in 1820, and 12,000 in 1831."[51] Sometimes the ranchers walked their own cows to the eastern cities for sale. More often they hired "drovers" who drove the cattle east on foot for a fee. Or the drovers bought the cattle themselves, frequently on credit, and then sold the cattle for a profit in the East.

Skaggs writes, "In 1817 a man identified only as Drenning drove 200 head of Ohio cattle to Manhattan, the first western beasts known to reach that market. The New York *Press* [*sic*] reported: 'They appear as fresh as if just taken off one of our Long Island farms. When it is recollected that they have been driven nearly one thousand miles, this fact will be considered a very remarkable one.'"[52] Drovers often collected cattle from various ranchers and herds. Although they walked anywhere from one hundred to one thousand cows on a trip, the drovers usually only had one or two humans and a couple of shepherd dogs to assist them. Walking during the day, the drovers would stop to rest for the night often renting overnight pasture from farmers along the way "for as much as five cents a head per night."[53]

Some of the drovers did very well. For example, Skaggs notes that the "net profit on an 1805 drive from the Scioto River to Baltimore reportedly was thirty-two dollars a head" and the drive included two hundred cows.[54] Herding two hundred cattle for thirty-two dollars a head makes for a lot of money in the terms of 1805.

Train Travel

Early on, as the frontier moved west, the cows had further to walk east at the end of their lives. However, with time, the markets moved west too, chasing the frontier and the cows, developing in the new urban areas birthed by the new western frontier. And the cow transportation changed as well. Some cows traveled by boat to new meatpacking centers in Ohio. Other cows, raised during the Civil War, traveled by flatboat on the Ohio and Mississippi rivers to New Orleans. Eventually, railroads became an option. Early on, railroads were too expensive for cattle ranchers. Skaggs explains, "In 1855 the Erie Railroad charged as much as $12.50 a head to ship live cattle from Columbus, Ohio, to New York, which was approximately one-third more than the cost of professional drovers, whose leisurely pace allowed animals to fatten en route."[55]

Another problem with railroads was that they sometimes overcrowded the cows in the boxcars, at times hurting or killing them. Skaggs writes, "Most area farmers consequently preferred to sell their animals to emerging meatpacking plants in Ohio, where prices invariably were lower than those along the East Coast, rather than pay high freight rates or trust unknown drovers with a whole year's production of animals."[56]

Yet over time, the railroads increasingly saved cows a long death march, carrying the cows to their slaughter instead. In 1830, the United States contained 23 miles of railroad track. Thirty years later in 1860, this had grown to 30,626 miles.[57] Most of these tracks were east of the Mississippi River and linked most of the cows east of the Mississippi to the slaughterhouses and meatpacking plants on that side of the river.

After the Civil War, cattle finally began to regularly ride trains as the trains started taking their bovine passengers more seriously and offered them safer trips. They also organized with one another to avoid rate wars where cattle shippers played them off of each other to get the cheapest rates.

Railroads played a central role in the consolidation of the meat industry. They made long-distance, relatively fast, and safe travel possible in cold as well as hot weather. Trains allowed animals to move across bodies of water and other natural obstacles that would have stopped the beasts on foot. With trains, the Ohio basin's market could open beyond its primary focus, the South.[58]

Railroad executives themselves ran cattle on railroad land. And they were not alone among elites buying into the cattle business. Many wealthy people put money into cattle ranching in the late 1880s. For example, Skaggs notes:

> Union Pacific executives Oliver Ames, Sidney Dillon, and Thomas Durant ran cattle on railroad land along the North Platte in Nebraska, and New York Central principal William Vanderbilt owned a ranch in Colorado. Breakfast-food baron C. W. Post profitably operated a 250,000-acre ranch in Texas ... *New York Herald* publisher James Gordon Bennett, Jr., bought a Wyoming spread, and Chicago merchant Marshall Field invested in the Pratt-Farris Cattle Co., which operated in Nebraska, Wyoming, and the Dakotas.[59]

So generation after generation of cows moved slowly west, pushing the frontier ahead of them, and growing fat off the land as they immigrated. And they birthed babies. And they nuzzled them and nursed them and protected their babies. And then after some years, the cows' lives ended, often by making another journey, this one east on foot or by train to the slaughterhouses.

With industrialization came industrialized slaughter and the slaughterhouses. Slaughterhouses meant centralization; meat packers began to kill and pack more and more animals at a given location. The first technology to mass-produce meat—that is, process live animal bodies into cuts of meat, in mass—developed with hogs in Cincinnati or as it was called, "Porkopolis." Ross writes, "By 1850, Ohio alone accounted for about a third of all American meat packing." There were a variety of reasons that early mass-produced meat originated in Cincinnati, Ohio. Industrialization coincided with rapidly increasing corn production in the United States. And Ohio had "ready access to surplus corn" to feed and fatten the animals before slaughter. Like cows, pigs fattened nicely on corn. Indeed, "hogs came to be widely regarded as a form of condensed corn, and the most efficient way to market the grain." Also, Ohio held the advantage of the heavily populated cotton plantations of the lower Mississippi. These offered a keen market for the meat from Ohio. Further, Ohio had access to capital from Boston packinghouses to fund the operations.[60]

Refrigerated Cows

By preventing decay, refrigeration revolutionized the meat industry. Refrigeration burst through the limits of space and time, allowing dead cow body parts to travel all over the nation and the world. With this, the industry became even more centralized. Prerefrigeration, lots of little businesses and private families raised, killed, and ate their meat locally with little time between the killing and the eating for most meats (pork being the exception). With refrigeration, suddenly the meat industry owned more time. Post death and preconsumption, meat could travel great distances and wait safely for lengthy periods before being eaten.

Refrigeration propelled the mass production of the meat of cows because it bought beef the time preserved pork already had. And *fresh* cow meat could "effectively compete with pork in taste and especially in price." Ross notes, "American swine were immediately placed at a severe disadvantage because they had never been bred to produce *fresh* meat, but rather to yield flesh which was ideally suited to salting and curing and which was fairly soft and fatty."[61] With refrigeration, "meat packing—although still heavily involved in pork—shifted its focus, as it entered the era of corporate capitalism."[62]

Refrigeration allowed for more than the mere mass slaughter and packing of cow meat. It also saved, Ross notes, "the expense of shipping the 35–40% of a steer that was inedible."[63] Shipping one-third of each cow for no profit is a lot of unnecessary cow travel. And with the mass slaughter of cows came the consolidation of that inedible 35-40 percent of all those cows. That is a lot of excess cow. For example, one important meatpacking company, George Fowler, Son and Company in Kansas City, annually processed 10,000 cattle by 1886.[64] One-third of 10,000 makes for plenty of extra bovine body. From all that extra cow produced in centralized, organized locations developed the extremely lucrative by-products industry.

Before refrigeration pigs had been more economical than cows because humans could eat more of the animal. In contrast to the 70–75 percent of a pig that could be eaten, only 50–55 percent of a cow could be eaten.[65] With refrigeration and the increasing centralization of slaughter, meat packers found uses for that inedible cow. Ross writes, "In the Twin Cities market area in 1912, for example, a 1000-pound steer generated over 15 dollars in by-products, compared to just under a third that value from an equal weight in hogs." The most important pig by-product had been lard. This was slowly being "replaced as an illuminant and lubricant, by the increasing use of petroleum … while, in contrast, a rising demand for hides by Eastern manufacturers meant a market for more and more cattle."[66]

Containing Cows, Claiming Land

Wild or contained, cows seem to have remained fairly docile throughout the history of the beef industry. We humans count on that docility. Indeed, today, the very material with which we often contain cows, barbed wire, reflects the reality that they are generally gentle animals. Sociologist Reviel Netz explains that barbed wire was invented in 1874 after a device on sale at an agricultural fair—nails stuck into a wooden board to be attached to the head of wandering livestock—intrigued Joseph F. Glidden. Whenever the animal tried to press herself into a limited area, she would bring herself intense pain. The board with its nails replaced the presence of human beings. It was a punishing, portable wall demanding obedience. Glidden, recognizing its potential, improved upon this innovation. He took the nails off of the animal and put them on an actual wall, or really a fence. The fascinating part of this invention was its frailty. The fence, made of strands of wire with nails or barbs attached, is surprisingly insubstantial. But, as I said, humans count on the fact that cows are docile.[67]

The Great Plains offered an ocean-like expanse of land flowing seemingly without end or tree. If humans were crazy enough to try and fence in this dry ocean, they needed a material like barbed wire to do it. Upon its invention, barbed wire quickly became available across the United States. Skaggs writes that "competition between rival manufacturers drove its price down to $1.80 per 100 pounds in 1880 from $20 in 1874."[68]

The fencing started largely to mark property rather than to contain cattle. Against appearances, neither oceans nor plains are infinite. Eventually, the cattle ranchers reached the end of the land. Skaggs claims:

> Inevitably the range-cattle industry overexpanded, in the process heightening competition for the land. The story had been much the same since colonial times: livestock raisers cropped public forage until pushed farther west by the advancing farmer; however, during the heyday of the cattle ranch the free grass finally played out, forcing herdsmen to become landowners to survive. Conflicts between competing claimants pitted rancher against rancher, drover against shepherd, herdsman against farmer, and corporation against individual.[69]

This competition sparked barbed wire's popularity. Many used it to fence in land they owned or leased. Others used barbed wire to fence in land belonging to someone else or land in the public domain. In Wyoming, where I grew up, "the Swan Land and Cattle Company, Ltd., of Edinburgh bought a half million acres from the Union Pacific and fenced in a half-million more." When the government investigated such land grabbing in Wyoming, they found that "between 4.4 million and 7.3 million acres of the public domain were looted by livestock raisers, principally cattlemen."[70]

Along with outright stealing land, cattle ranchers battled other cattle ranchers, farmers, and shepherds for land. Many cattle ranchers held prejudice against sheep and some attacked flocks. In one case in Wyoming, in 1889, a cattle rancher set fire to a sheep herder's pasture. Not only was damage done to the land, but the shepherd's child was badly burned as well.

Many cattle ranchers incorrectly believed that cattle would not eat grass where sheep had walked because of the smell of the sheep. Although that myth was false, sheep do graze grass closer to the earth.

If left in a pasture too long, they "could trample a pasture into dust, leaving nothing for bovines." Skaggs claims, "Many early flockmasters were tramps [*sic*] who moved on whenever the grass played out, unmindful of or uncaring about the denudation they left behind."[71]

My grandmother's father, Tulesis, was a sheepherder. Before my Gram married a Wyoming cattleman, she grew up in a small town just across the border of Wyoming in Nebraska. I do not know how he treated the land, but according to my grandmother, he was a good man. He did not, she told me once, make a profit off of the war like many did. When my Gram married she moved across the state border to Kidron. Her father died before I was born, but her mother, my great-grandmother May, lived well into my childhood. I remember my grandmother visiting her regularly. I remember that she needed a caregiver in the end of her life; she needed but did not want one. She used to send the caregiver outside for something and then lock her out of the house, refusing to let her back in. She lived in a beautiful old house with a large porch. I think Tulesis built that house, or maybe his father did. After May died, it was torn down so that someone could put a fast-food restaurant there.

Visiting Little America

I loved my grandmother Clarke. I loved to be with her. In the summer I would go to visit her at my grandparents' house in Kidron, Wyoming, for two weeks. These two weeks were extraordinary. They were special. I wanted to stay forever.

For some of my summer visits, my father would fly me to Kidron in his little plane. Sometimes he would drive me. A couple of times he only drove me to Spokane and my grandparents came to meet me, to pick me up there. We would meet at the Little America. So, because everything having to do with my grandmother turned to special, Little America became a special place. Going there was a treat, a luxury to be relished, like a candy bar at the movies.

Of course, Little America was unique in my experience. Grand Junction, Wyoming, where we lived, was a town of 15,000 to 20,000 people and was not on a major interstate. It was not large or central enough to have a Little America. In contrast, Spokane was big, almost a real city. Spokane had a shopping mall and movie theaters with several different screens showing several different movies at once. So it made sense that Spokane, with all its wonders, would also have a Little America. With seemingly no irony, Little America with its hotel, gas station, gift shop, restaurant, and many other exciting things, existed because of and for consumption. It was a place where travelers stopped on their way to other places. It promised potential, like a car trip. And it was thrilling to a small girl from a small town in Wyoming. When we arrived, I would feel a rush of excitement.

At Little America you could do just about everything a person might want to do. You could buy gas for your car. You could stay the night. There was a restaurant where you could get all kinds of things including apple pie, french fries, and milkshakes where they didn't just give you the glass, they gave you the silver mixer with all the extra milkshake too. There was a gift shop that displayed the most wonderful stuffed animals I had ever seen. There was a fancy ladies room. When you went in, you first went through a lobby with cushioned seats and mirrors, and then another room with handwashing sinks and yet more mirrors, all before you finally came to the room with the toilets. Little America was full of possibility.

When we went to special places my father treated me kindly. Everything was good. Arriving at Little America we would park the car and enter the main building, up the steps covered in red carpet and through the big front doors. Then we would go left, into the restaurant to wait for my grandparents. I can still picture my grandmother, see her in my mind, when she came to pick me up at Little America. She would come with my grandfather. He died several years ago. But then, when he was alive and she not bedridden, he would do all the long distance driving. Women only drove in town. Men drove for trips. This was how it was. It was one of those things that never made sense, but it didn't matter because it simply was that way.

So my grandmother did not come to pick me up alone at Little America. She came in the passenger seat, with my grandfather driving. They would enter the restaurant looking for us. Seeing my grandmother, my whole self filled with gladness. She would smile at me. She did not smile a big open smile. Just like she never laughed out loud. I guess it would not be tasteful. I was never quite sure what the rules were exactly. But they were there and this was one of them. Yet she did smile at me, and I knew she too was glad.

To greet me or to say good-bye, my grandmother would give me a kiss. Well, it wasn't really a kiss. It was a sort-of-kiss. She would put her cheek out, touching me on my cheek, then moving quickly away. She always smelled good. My grandfather greeted me by pulling my hair. Sort of gently, but not really. He would ask me something, to which I did not know the answer and he didn't listen anyhow.

Soon, it was time to go. I would sit in the back seat of their always new, always fancy and big car. Between my grandfather's driving and the new car smell, I would feel carsick the whole way to Kidron. But I did not complain. Complaining was bad, not complaining was good, and I wanted to please my grandmother. She would periodically smile back at me from the front seat. The drive from Spokane to Kidron is one-and-one-half hours long. Only a little bit of it is on interstate, most is on a small rural highway threading together small rural towns. It is beautiful. The sky is so big in Wyoming, so very big that many things can be happening all at one time within it. Underneath such endless sky, one is especially small. And it is okay. One feels held by that sky. One knows that all will be well.

This I Know

It's funny I forgot this year. Ash Wednesday is still my mother's favorite religious day. Like much in the Catholic tradition, it is a day whose symbolism is deeply rooted in the earth. From ashes we come and to ashes we shall return. We were Catholic. For my grandmother Clarke, it would have been unforgivable not to go to Mass on Ash Wednesday. In fact, both my grandmothers used to go to Mass every day. In our Irish Catholic family, religion was a place where women had some power. I guess it had to do with that earthy thing. Blood and bodily pain were women's domain, both dirty and awesome, animal and Godlike at once. It was known that women were especially connected to God.

Men, on the other hand, they ran things. While women lived in the day-to-day simple and mundane rituals of life, men lived in the *world*. They made things happen. My grandfather was a powerful man. In the family, and outside too, he held respect. He owned places and things in the world, land and cattle and people's jobs. He grew wheat and corn, and raised beef. To me, they were cows, soft and brown, thoughtful creatures with big sad eyes. But to my grandfather, and he knew, they were beef. New calves, yearlings, two-year olds ready for slaughter, breed cows were all potential meat. And meat was money, money and power. This was the language of his world.

He taught me things, my grandfather. He showed me how to eat a baked potato, deep yellow with half a stick of butter and lots of salt. From him, I learned that to order steak rare was not ladylike, but medium did a disservice to our ranching family. I ate my steak medium rare to make my grandfather proud. My brother, who was adopted, ate his steak well done, a sure sign that his blood was not the same as ours. My grandfather, although polite to my brother, never quite accepted him. For family, next to business, was everything. And like business, you were born into the family or you were not. Success ran in the blood preordained.

Yet, I was a girl. And while my blood was his, I could not share his world. When I visited my grandparents, I spent time with my grandmother. She opened her life to me. And for a time, I would rest there.

My grandmother had a rose garden. This I know. When I think of her, I remember a smell both elegant and distant, like a rose. My grandmother was elegant and distant. My grandmother did not hold me. She never touched me. I don't know what her skin felt like—only that she had spots, brown spots, on her hands. And, I know, she disliked the spots intensely. To her they were no accomplishment of growing old, mark of a life well lived. For her, the spots were dirty, stains that could not be removed. They were like shame.

My grandmother had a rose garden in her backyard. I would follow her there under the pretense of helping. She knew many things about roses. She knew where they should be cut, and when, so as not to hurt the plant. She knew how to make a yard quiet, and time stop, so that the roses would grow in abundance. She knew how to gather them, put them together in a bowl so that they were beautiful, so beautiful your breath halted for a second when you saw them. They would fill a room with their rich scent, both elegant and distant. Roses are not like daisies. One has to be careful when picking a rose, with its sharp, strong thorns. Roses are not like daisies, overjoyed to be alive, reaching eagerly for the sun. Roses demand a certain awe. Maybe my grandmother loved roses because she saw herself in them. Or maybe it was because they reminded her of her God, who was also awesome, who was also distant. My grandmother lived in very certain spaces. She lived in her rose garden. She lived in her kitchen. And she lived in her church. Hers was a world where women had their place. And men, men had everywhere else. Luckily, women got God. Although it was only because men did not need him. They were in charge anyhow.

My grandmother's God was awesome. His house was at the Catholic church. And he, like my grandmother, was removed. While always present, he was never familiar. We did not discuss God. To speak of God in daily conversation was something worse than disrespect. Yet, even so, the silence granted God was not unusual. My family was filled with silences. Gaping quiet. Empty places. God existed somewhere there, in that silence.

Chapter 5

The Production of Girl Life and the Lives of Girls

In this chapter, I explore trauma and its normalizing effects in my own childhood. I also examine the ways that my experience reflects the larger normative culture as described by the radical feminist movement of the 1970s. In my childhood, violence normalized. It worked to gender me as a normative girl. I became quiet, accepting, submissive, disembodied and disassociated from my body, without sexual feeling, and ashamed. Along with violence, trauma saturated my childhood. And the sexual clung to and burst from my gendered experiences of both. For me, becoming girl meant succumbing to another's sexuality. Being-girl was a matter of no-longer-mattering, in both senses of the word. My girl-experience was that of no-longer-being-embodied. Instead my form became the surface for the pleasure of another.

My sister, Annie, and I share a dream-memory, or perhaps merely a dream, or perhaps actually a memory. It is hard to say. The dream-memory happened to each of us when we were three. Or it didn't happen. It is hard to say.

Being three years apart, of course we were not three at the same time. I was three and staying with my grandparents in Kidron while my mother was giving birth to my sister, Annie. She was three when I was six, and for some reason she was visiting my grandparents in Kidron at three, just like I had done, only this time there was no little sister being born.

The Dream-Memory

Clarke may be the closest thing I can find to a starting point. Everyone else seemed to have a reason that came before them. My father, for example, had Clarke. But Clarke, Clarke it seems to me was simply cruel. Clarke was cruelty out of nowhere. Or maybe the cruelty came from the world. Maybe the world rotted Clarke. Maybe the job of living was too much for him and he gave in to killing instead. I don't know.

But he was cruel. No one said it. That was not allowed. Maybe no one even thought it. Except for me.

Clarke was the king. And everyone pretended everything was okay. Everyone pretended not to see. Or maybe, maybe, they were not pretending. Maybe if one does not see for so long, too long, generations, one loses the capacity to see. Or maybe blindness simply ran in the family. I don't know.

But I do know that something, something, was wrong with Clarke. And Clarke brought wrongness with him. He spread it everywhere.

My father did not tell me stories about Clarke. He just gave me the party line. Clarke he held up as an example of how The Father must be treated. One did not question Clarke. One did not question the father. This never-to-be-questioned status was a birthright, a birthright of the father. Even God said so.

I only heard a few stories about Clarke. I heard them from my mother and my grandmother. Behind the curtain shielding what was, from what was real, my grandmother slipped me some truth. My grandmother told me a few stories, a few stories about Clarke.

And the sad thing is that it's over. And yet it's not. My childhood was a horrible place to be. And it is over. It is over and yet I do not know how to leave it behind. That is the sad thing. I am not sure how to live in this world. I am not sure how to live with what happened. I am not sure that I want to.

I can tell you what I want, what I really want. I want for none of this to have happened. I want a different set of memories. I am not who I want to be.

Will you tell me how to live with this? Can you, can you tell me how to live?

Out of Nowhere

Here is something I remember. It is a dream or a memory, and it is strange. And it is out of nowhere. And I am so afraid. The word, afraid, cannot cover what I feel. Here is something I remember.

I am small, maybe three years old or so. And I am sitting on a tall wooden chair. It is an adult chair, and I am a small girl. The chair is much too big for me. I want to tell you that they had tied me to the chair. But I am afraid you won't believe me. Even so, I think they did. And everywhere is dark. I can barely see. And suddenly a strange man, although maybe not so strange, in some way I recognize him as the doctor who lived down the street from my grandparents, the doctor who was friends with Clarke, suddenly this man pierces me with a needle. He grips me tightly to hold me still and pierces my arm with a needle. He gives me a shot. And then all is gray. And then all is blank. That is all I remember.

Men Work

My grandmother said that maybe they were too hard on my father. I wondered who "they" entailed. It seemed she meant herself and my grandfather, Clarke. Yet I think the "they" was really just Clarke. About this, about Clarke, she only told odds and ends, no complete stories, no full information. She said my grandfather used to beat my father. Maybe it was too much she said. Maybe. And, she said, my father had terrible allergies to hay. He had spring fever. But not the regular kind. It got so bad his face swelled up, and he almost could not see. And in those days, there weren't all the different allergy medications that we have now. I myself am a big user of allergy medications. I, like my father, have spring fever. I am particularly allergic to spring in New York City, I guess because it is not my home. But for me now, there is no home. So I take the medication and wait for the allergies to pass. My father could only wait. He did not have the medication to take. The best thing for him would have been to stay away from hay. But Clarke did not care about the best thing for him. Like I said, Clarke was cruel. Clarke believed young men should work. Clarke believed young men should work for their father. Clarke believed men did not stop work because of a little allergy. To be a man meant to work and be strong, no matter what. And so, at Clarke's salebarn, surrounded by hay, my father worked his way through sickness, he worked his way through spring.

The Dream-Memory Happened Like This

Once when I was very small, Clarke did something cruel to me as well. Was this why my grandmother had me stay in her room with her? I don't know. I don't know if it ever happened again. I don't know if anything else happened. I don't know if it happened, at all. I don't know. I don't know.

You probably won't believe me. You probably won't believe what I have to say. But I will tell you anyhow. At least one time, Clarke did something cruel to me. It happened like this.

When I was almost three, in May, my sister was born in the hospital in Grand Junction. My father, being the father, could not take care of us. He could not take care of my brother. He could not take care of me. He was the father. So he took my mother's dog to the vet and had the dog put to sleep. That dog was named Tinker, and he was my mother's favorite dog ever. She really loved that dog. But my father being the father could not take care of a dog. He had important things to do. So he killed the dog and he took my brother and me to my grandparents' house. I guess my brother and I were lucky. We were lucky that my grandparents agreed to take us. We were luckier than that poor little dog, my mother's favorite dog ever, Tinker. He was such a good dog, my mother said. And so smart. Well, my father left us at my grandparents' house for two weeks. I don't remember my brother being there. I thought I was there all alone. But my mother says he was there. And my brother does not remember.

My mother remembers looking out her hospital window and watching us drive by. My father, my brother Martin, who we called Marty then, and me. Anne, who we called Annie, was in the hospital with my mother. She had just been born. And I guess the dog was already dead. My mother says she watched us drive by from her hospital window. She says she waved to us. Somehow I remember watching her disappear, her face in the window, in the hospital, everything becoming smaller behind us as we drive away. Although maybe I don't really remember, maybe I just think I do.

My mother told me she did not know he was going to take us away. She did not know he was going to kill her dog either. He didn't tell her. He just did these things. That's how it was. He was the father. My mother cried when she told me this story. She cried. And she said, he could have let you talk to me on the phone. He could have let you say good-bye. When she told me, I cried too. She cried for us and I cried for her, her and her little dog, her little dog, Tinker. My father at this point had already become cruel. He was young, only 29. He was younger than I am now. Yet it was too late. For him, it was too late. He was already cruel like my grandfather.

My brother, Martin, was the first grandchild to my father's parents. I was the second. We made my father's parents into grandparents. Before us, they were only parents. My grandmother was glad to be a grandmother. And my brother called her Gram. My brother named my grandmother. He named her Gram. But Clarke did not want to be Grandfather. He named himself with his last name. He named himself Clarke. And so we called them Gram and Clarke.

And my father left us there. My father left us with Gram and Clarke for two weeks. He had important things to do. And my mother had just given birth. Annie had just been born. My mother has a picture from that time, in our family album. It was taken of me at my grandparents' during those two weeks, those two weeks when my father left us there, when Annie had just been born. In the photograph, I am standing alone, in front of what were probably the living room curtains, and I am crying. I am crying and crying. They say I cried the whole time I was there. I cried and cried.

And I didn't remember. Until four years ago, I didn't remember anything of that trip. And then four years ago, I did. It was a dream that I remembered. Or it was a memory. I cannot say.

I already told you that my grandfather was cruel. He was cruel. But beyond that I don't know who he was. I never knew him. I never knew that man. There were strange bits and pieces that burst through the story we lived with from day to day. Like once, when I was talking with my aunts in my grandmother's kitchen, some of my boy cousins came running in from downstairs, downstairs past where The Girls' Room waited, downstairs again to the basketball court that my grandfather had in the basement. My cousins were shouting excitedly that they had found Ku Klux Klan robes in my grandfather's basement. Really, they said, *really*. They were thrilled with their discovery. The aunts hushed them, hurriedly, moving them back out of the kitchen to silence. Later when we, some of us cousins, went back to look at their discovery, the robes were gone.

My grandfather gave me shiny new silver dollars when I came to visit. He pulled my hair. He asked, what do you know? Only my grandmother had an answer to that question. She would respond, it takes a big dog to weigh a hundred pounds.

When I visited my grandmother, she would take me shopping in Salida. We would make a day trip in her fancy car. We would drive to Salida. Salida was in Nebraska just across the Wyoming border. Salida was where my grandmother grew up. She had been a little girl there. Compared to Kidron, Salida was big. It even had a country club. On our shopping trip, our special trip to Salida, my grandmother would buy me a whole new outfit and she would take me out to lunch. Usually we went to eat at the country club. It was a special day, just she and I. And I loved it.

My grandmother would buy me a brand new outfit at the Salida children's store. The lady at the store knew us. She knew my grandmother, and she was very nice to us. She was very nice in a way that nobody was to my mother when my mother went shopping. I noticed the difference. It made me feel both good and bad at once. I loved being with my grandmother. I loved being special. But, nonetheless, the lady's niceness made me ache inside. It made me ache for my mother.

My grandmother liked girl clothes. She liked lacy dresses and shoes with bows and ribbons, clothes that made things clear. In them, everybody knew you were a girl. Everybody knew what was what. Unfortunately, I on the other hand, I did not like girl clothes. I liked clothes that one did not have to keep track of. I liked clothes that took little effort when they were, and when they weren't, on one's body. I did not like ribbons. This was a problem. I hated to disappoint my grandmother.

When we got home from our shopping trip, our day that always went too fast, I would try on my clothes for Clarke. I didn't want to do this. But my grandmother asked me to, so I would. And Clarke would comment. And then it was over. The day, the special shopping day, but also my contact with Clarke, was over. This was really the only contact I had with Clarke. Like I told you, I really never knew my grandfather.

And then, four years ago, I remembered a dream. Or a memory. I remembered a dream-memory of what had happened when I was three and staying with my grandparents, when I was staying with my grandparents because my sister, Annie, had just been born and my father being the father could not take care of us. I remembered and I didn't. I cannot be sure. I remembered, but not like a photograph. I remembered but I cannot take the memory out of my pocket. I remembered but I cannot show you the memory and say, see, here it is. I have nothing real to show, only vagueness. And yet, I remembered. And while you probably will not believe me, I remember nonetheless. I remember now.

I remembered being small and in a room. And the room was actually a little barn or shed that stood in front of Clarke's salebarn. Other than this memory, I have never been in that shed. But the shed exists. It exists outside of my memory. It is real and can be found in front of what used to be my grandfather's salebarn, until he sold it years ago. It is still there unless they tore it down. And I was on a chair. It is a tall wooden chair. And I am a small girl. The chair is much too big for me. And there was a table, long and wooden. And men were standing around the table and I was at one end on the chair and the men had funny outfits on with hoods. And I think the doctor was there, the doctor who lived down the street from my grandparents, the doctor who was friends with Clarke. And my grandfather stood at the other end of the table. I think it was my grandfather standing there, holding a kitten. And he killed the kitten with a knife. And they painted the blood around the room. I was too scared to cry. I remember.

Trauma and Time

My story, as told, mimics the lived experience of trauma circling around and through tone, place, and familial generations. In my experience, trauma cuts through time and reoccurs as a compulsive repetition of the traumatic moment, of the violence. The traumatic experience happens in and is made up of bodies as much as it is held in other spaces, times, and places.

I tell my childhood story much as it was and continues to be experienced by me, almost as though time does not move forward. In contrast, the story I tell of US beef cattle moves chronologically through time starting with the cows' arrival in North America, moving forward to the industrialization of the meat industry, and a present-day look at the lives of cows, their deaths in slaughterhouses, and what becomes of them once dead. The story from my childhood circles around on itself, with no particular beginning and no real ending. This circling time represents, I believe, the experience of trauma as time*less*, in the sense of always-there, as fresh and vivid and gripping as the violent gendered and sexual acts that birthed the trauma, indeed perhaps more present even than when the violence was experienced.

It was late at night. And we were little girls. My sister even smaller than I. My sister loved that cat. She loved that cat. Really, she had not much else to love. And he woke us up. And he brought us to the garage. I don't remember getting there. Instead, suddenly, in my mind, it is night and we are there, my sister and I, standing side by side.

During violence, the traumatized being often "shuts down," numbs out, or in a sense, leaves. While away, she stores the violent experience in her being until a safer time to reexperience it, and often, reexperience it again and again and again. Trauma involves living caught in the past, and in particular, caught in a past moment of violence, or perhaps, merely the moments of life surrounding violence. The past moment plays over and over again like a broken record. And the traumatized person experiences that moment viscerally as a pain or a smell, a sound or a vision.[1] Or rather, to the extent that the event overwhelmed and overwhelms, one does not (re)experience the traumatic moment but instead circles around the experience compulsively and repetitively.

In remembering how, 33 years ago, my father gutted my sister's beloved childhood cat in front of us in a drunken rage, I circle around the violence remembering the events and affect leading up to and following it without ever fully knowing, mastering, moving through and beyond, or releasing the experience. It grips me, and I experience aspects of the event again and again and again, sweeping over me, as though they were actually occurring in the now. Caruth writes that "these repetitions are particularly striking because they seem not to be initiated by the individual's own acts but rather appear as the possession of some people by a sort of fate, a series of painful events to which they are subjected, and which seem to be entirely outside their wish or control."[2]

In turn, my father's violence was inextricably connected to his experience and expression of manhood. That night, when he killed my sister's cat, and so many other things as well, he shouted at us, or perhaps at someone we could not see; "I am a man! I am a man!"

In my experience of manhood, in my family, being a man meant rupturing the other, bursting through barriers of skin and flesh in violence, all too often sexual. To some extent, I think this reflected manhood in the larger normative culture. Going from boy to man, to being a "real man," meant taking on a never-ending struggle to prove oneself until finally, one did reach the end. And the only end to this was death. For men, real men, there was no stopping during life. Whatever one might want, once obtained, no longer meant much at all. The real thing was always another thing, something else. There was no point of saturation, no stopping, no lasting experience of enough, no money, no cow, no production, no others' deaths, no sex enough. No end to this hunger.

Beef reflects this orientation. The beef industry epitomizes my family's, our culture's desire for, our pressing need for more, and again, more. In sharp contrast to raising cattle, my grandmother grew roses. Her roses contained their meaning in the now. My grandfather's cows were for something else. They were for what they would become, meat. And money.

Trauma and the Radical Feminist Movement

Now I want to engage my experience and thinking with a broader conversation. The radical feminist movement of the 1970s happened simultaneous to my childhood. This movement brought normalizing gendered violence and trauma to national attention. Radical feminists, a prominent faction of the second wave feminist movement, argued that girls become girls, in part, through violence and its effects, trauma. Violence normalizes as it produces girlness. Violence/trauma also plays a clear role in the political economic reproduction of gendered power (and the power of humans over other animals). Thus, through violence, gendered power is reproduced.

The radical feminists brought the reality of gendered violence into mainstream consciousness. Suddenly we saw it, and we saw it everywhere: domestic violence, sexual harassment, rape, child sexual abuse, incest.[3] We recognized violence and trauma at the heart of gendered power, at the heart of normative gender.[4]

In 2007, I wrote about this movement: "Radical feminism argued that intimate relationships, and the ways those relationships were lived in the everyday through institutions like the family, were inextricably connected to larger gendered systems of power. Men and boys had power over women and girls." The radical feminists claimed that everyday institutions of our society, like the "traditional" nuclear family, played an important role in the oppression of women and girls. And although the radical feminists believed that gendered oppression happened through other forms of power including economic, psychological, and political, violence was the ultimate, bottom line defense. Incest and child sexual abuse exemplified this perfectly.

> Incest was a prime example of male oppression, often enacted through male control over, and abuse of, female bodies ... Ultimately, radical feminists argued that incest was more than simply a result of the patriarchy; it was a means to *re-create* the patriarchy. Girls learned to be girls—they became girls—through a socialization process that included male violation of their bodies and selves.[5]

About incest, prominent radical feminist psychiatrist and trauma researcher, Judith Lewis Herman argued, "Female children are regularly subjected to sexual assaults by adult males who are part of their intimate social world." She continued, "The aggressors are not outcasts and strangers; they are neighbors, family friends, uncles, cousins, stepfathers, and fathers. To be sexually exploited by a known and trusted adult is a central and formative experience in the lives of countless women."[6] Herman claimed:

> Father-daughter incest is not only the type of incest most frequently reported but also represents a paradigm of female sexual victimization. The relationship between father and daughter, adult male and female child, is one of the most unequal relationships imaginable. It is no accident that incest occurs most often precisely in the relationship where the female is most powerless.[7]

Trauma and Its Other (Possible) Effects

The radical feminists presented a worldview where violence and trauma both produce and reproduce gendered social power. Violence normalizes through reproducing taken-for-granted male power. In my experience, this is an adept description of violent effects, albeit perhaps not the full story. In this section, I also want to note that the violence I experienced, and perhaps violence in the larger culture as well, seemed to play multiple roles. It seemed that my father's out-of-control brutality, springing from his own traumatized history, also pulled apart our world, and did so in a way that opened possibilities. The trauma, and the repetition of that traumatic experience in my everyday life, not only normalized—and built a social order—but also ruptured the order of things, bursting through what political scientist Timothy Pachirat calls the "zones of confinement"[8] to open to something else. In some way, hidden or confined everyday violence and trauma not only reproduced but also challenged normalizing power.

Somehow life pushes for itself. It demands. It demands freedom.

I wonder: Outside of my family, like the panic disorders examined by Jackie Orr,[9] how might the crazy, surprising, unexpected nature of violence and trauma pull apart the management of populations, bursting through the seams of the expected, and through trauma opening up the zones that confine? Trauma like, indeed as a manifestation of, life itself at times explodes beyond the reach of, or perhaps through, power's subsumption of it. Using the example of disease, as an example of life itself, Shukin notes that in the case of animal capital,

> while the balance of power seems, ominously, to be all on the side of capital, it is crucial to also recognize the amplified vulnerability of capitalism in tautological times. Indeed, novel diseases erupting out of the closed loop of animal capital—mad cow disease, avian influenza—are one material sign of how the immanent terrain of market becomes susceptible, paradoxically, to the pandemic potential of "nature."[10]

Here Shukin argues that nature sometimes, in someway, rebels against capital, albeit perhaps accidentally.

Unlike the negative effects of disease-disrupting power, trauma has been both deeply damaging, and in someway in favor of, life, my life. Trauma has, in some small part, expressed Deleuze's "obstinate, stubborn and indomitable will to live."[11] In my experimental writing, violence/trauma plays diverse roles in the reproduction of life and in the reproduction of normalizing power. In part, violence seems to move beyond the making of power, in the making of a docile gendered girl population, and challenge it. In my family, violence/trauma—in both its mundane everydayness and in its shocking out-of-the ordinariness—*is* primarily, but not merely, an instrument of power. In part, this is because violence is also a traumatic response to, rather than merely a result of, discipline and normalization, and perhaps in this, a (traumatized) form of resistance. In my memoir writing, I wonder how—and I write this question around the edges of the story—these mundane, everyday forms of confined violence and its traumatic effects disrupt and challenge normalizing power.

If nothing else, it is the trauma in its day-to-day impact on my life that pushed me to face my own history. Really, it left me no choice.

My pain motivated me to find a way through and out of it. It might not have been this way, this way that led to here and now. It might have been another way, perhaps my father's way, perhaps Erin's way, but staying there, in that suffering, was not a viable option.

In another place, in another set of memories, clarity might not matter. I mean, really, if all were well, then who cares what happened. If all were well, then what happened, and other such details, are insignificant. But, all was not well. All was not well. This much I know. And it is the pain that makes me push the edges of our family truth.

A Special Occasion Dinner

As I said, sometimes my grandparents picked me up at Little America and drove me to Kidron to visit them. When we arrived in Kidron, my grandfather would drive us up the driveway of their house to let my grandmother and me out. He had to go to the salebarn. He was a man and had important things to do. I didn't mind. My grandmother and I entered the house through the side door in the garage. The house was big, quiet, and filled with her presence. It was a house that held many memories. I do not know the memories. They are not mine. But I know they were there in that house, everywhere. That house let go of nothing.

My grandmother's house was where my father, her first son, grew up. It was where all five of her sons and no daughters grew. My grandmother wanted a daughter. Even though boys are better, she still wanted at least one daughter. She wanted a daughter and had only sons, five sons named Simon, Matthew, Nathan, Aldous, and Bartholomew. Simon, Matthew, and Bartholomew are names of three of the disciples. Aldous was named after my grandfather, whose name was Aldous, even though we called him Clarke. And as one might expect, Aldous was the especially crazy one. My mother thinks that when you give a child someone else's name, you give much more than just the name. In some way, the child takes on that person's path in the world, his legacy. My mother does not want us, her children, to name our own children after her or other people in the family. But for my grandmother's five sons, it is too late. Uncle Matt was not only named after a disciple but also Gram's brother, who was a priest, and probably named after a disciple himself. And I don't know where Uncle Nat's name came from. Maybe that is why he was the lost one.

When I was a child, I went to visit Gram for two weeks in the summer. I am not sure when this ritual started and became official, an event to be counted on. But it did, at least for awhile. And yet, then, everything changes, even official events, and somewhere in the years I stopped going. At some point I stopped going to stay with Gram for two weeks, by myself, every summer. The ritual ended.

And now I have not seen my grandmother for too many years. I went once, for a day. It was in the fall of 1993 and my grandmother was old. Although she had not stopped remembering, as she later did, nonetheless one of us had changed too much. As she looked at me I knew she did not recognize me. I was not the one she remembered. She did not know who I was.

But when I was a child I would go to visit her for two weeks every summer. I would go by myself. And the time there, with my grandmother, was delicious. Every moment I held onto too tightly, so that it went even sooner than it might have otherwise. This is something I still do. Not everything has changed.

When we first entered her house, after being dropped off by my grandfather, I would be filled with recognition. Her house was familiar, yet always, somehow, new. Like Little America, but better, it was rich with potential.

The first room you entered, from the garage door on the side of the house, was the dining room. It was a room to be used only for special occasions. It was a luxury room. There was a big wooden dining room table in the middle of the room with a large crystal chandelier hanging over it. When all the family came over for a special occasion meal, the table would grow larger to accommodate us. It had big fancy wooden chairs with velvet cushions and very high backs all around it. When I sat in one of those chairs, I could rest my back and my neck and my head and still have chair, reaching up above me, leftover. The chairs were big and I was small.

On one side of the room, the side you faced when you came in from the garage, there was a wall-length, ceiling-high cupboard, just for dishes. My grandmother had lots of dishes. They came in sets from all over the world. When my grandmother napped, sometimes I would spend an afternoon looking at those dishes, imagining whose dreams they held. They were so fancy, so perfect. Maybe for my grandmother, having those dishes made everything okay.

When we had big family dinners, often my grandmother would let me set the table. With some stipulations, I could even choose the dishes to be used. It was a big choice. In a way, choosing the dishes gave me some control over how things went, not just at the dinner, but in general. Choosing made me glad and worried both. Sometimes I would have the table all ready, and then, decide to switch the dishes. This was okay with my grandmother.

I loved setting the table. I knew how to put the knives facing in toward the plate, the salad forks outside of the dinner forks, and the spoons outside of the knives. My grandmother taught me other things too, like that the salt should always stay with the pepper, spoons should never be left in dishes, and where the different glasses go. These were things she knew and told me. And I still love setting the table.

When we had those big family meals, my grandmother would sit at one end of the table, near the kitchen door, and my grandfather would sit at the other end. Everybody else sat in-between. But the rule was that men had to sit next to women, and women next to men. It was a rule, so we followed it.

Once, before my mother left my father, when I was very small, my mother broke a rule at a family dinner. It was a rule that no one contradicted my grandfather. No one contradicted my father either, except my grandfather. This was how things were. If you were a man you could not be contradicted, except if you were a man younger than another man. The oldest man could contradict everyone freely, with no repercussions. As a little girl I couldn't contradict anyone, except my little sister. Which I did.

Anyhow, one time at a family dinner my mother contradicted my grandfather. He was not her father; he was my father's father. This made him even more important, and it made her contradiction even worse. My grandfather was talking, which my grandfather did. He talked, his sons responded, and we listened. Sometimes the women talked quietly among themselves. Well, when my mother contradicted my grandfather, my grandfather was talking. And everyone was listening. My grandfather was talking about the niggers. He was telling us about them, about things they do and do not do, about how they cannot be trusted. My grandfather was talking. And, suddenly, my mother contradicted him. In my mind I remember her standing up. Maybe she really pushed back that big chair and stood up at the dinner table. Or maybe she didn't. But either way, it was a kind of standing up because she interrupted my grandfather. And even worse, according to the rules, she told him what to do. Or rather, she told him what not to do. She told him not to use that word, that word nigger. She told him that maybe he believed in that word, but she didn't. She told him he could talk like he wanted at other times, but not in front of her children, which was us. She told him that she could not stop him from thinking that way, that way that he thought. But she did not want her children to learn his way. She did not want her children to learn this word, and believe it to be right.

One time, when I was grown, my mother told me that she worried it was all her fault. She told me that she worried my grandfather did what he did as revenge. She said maybe he did those horrible things, to my sister and me, as a way to get back at her. He never again used that word in front of us, at least not until I was much older and my mother was no longer around. And by then, I had learned to shudder at that word, to feel sick in my stomach at my grandfather's thinking. But my mother said that maybe instead of talking that way, talking poison, he got back at my mother for her contradiction in a way much worse than words.

When my grandfather finally died, it was because all that poison finally killed him. He rotted alive from the inside out. In the last two years of his life, he had a terrible rash. I never saw it because I was not visiting my grandparents anymore. But my brother told me that he had a terrible rash. The rash was very ugly and very painful. It covered his whole body. And there was nothing they could do about it. He took lots and lots of baths and tried all kinds of special ointments. But nothing helped. The doctors did not know why he had this rash. Or if they knew, they did not say. Maybe they too were afraid of my grandfather. As far as I know, my mother was the only one who ever contradicted him. My mother has always been brave, braver even than poison.

Now my grandfather is finally dead. He died in June of 1993. I think the date was June 6, but I cannot be sure. By that time I was already cut off from my family. I still write it in my datebook. I write "Clarke died in 1993" on June 6. Then I put a question mark because I am not sure of the exact date. But, at least, I know he's dead. At least I know he is dead. That I know.

On the Ability to See Rabbits: Stories Involving a Girl, Her Grandmothers, and Aging Vision

In my family, getting old means that one stops seeing rabbits. Somewhere in the time between the intense visceral delight of being small and resting one's eyes on a rabbit, and the quick flash or slow wear of years until old age, one loses one's capacity to see, really see, rabbits. Perhaps rabbits actually vanish from the list of things that old eyes can perceive. Or perhaps, too many matters dealt with, too much sadness, too much disappointment makes rabbits somehow blend into the background of one's days, so that by 60 or 70, they no longer appear amidst sidewalks and trees, bus stops and front doors, lawns and roads. One's eyes give up on rabbits. Or perhaps, in my family the bad habit of not seeing, not seeing most of what really happened around one, and instead, insisting on seeing many things that never happened, ends up rubbing off on one's ability to see rabbits. I do not know. Not yet old, I myself have always had a sharp eye when it comes to rabbits.

When I was a child, like many children, I loved rabbits. Really, I loved animals. I always wanted to bring them home with me. And I always had a few small creatures living in my room, this or that room, in this or that house, as my mother found our way out of our history and made a new life for us. Along with my Shetland pony Dolly, my cat Thomasina, and a dog that looked uncannily like a mop, named Mopsy, through my growing-up-years, I had innumerable hamsters, mice, parakeets, rabbits, lizards, goldfish, guppies, guinea pigs, gerbils, turtles, and a good number of baby birds that I found on the way home from school.

Once, when we were spending the weekend out at my father's cabin, I even caught a small snake. My father, his second wife Lydia, and I were out for a walk when the snake presented itself. I was so excited on the way home, I ran the whole way, holding the snake carefully. The poor snake, on the other hand, was so frightened it threw up on my brother, Lydia's son Timothy, as soon as I got it inside. I had to let it go. Sadly, I took it out to the back yard, near the little creek we had, and placed it on the ground, under some brush. I'm sorry little snake, I told it. I really did feel badly about making the snake sick with fear. I knew about that myself. The snake responded by slithering quickly away.

The First Rabbit: The Rabbit I Took Home

Another time, I caught a rabbit. It was soft and white. It, like the snake, was also afraid. But the rabbit did not throw up. Maybe this was because the rabbit was somewhat more accustomed to human beings. In contrast, I think I may have been the small snake's first human encounter. Unfortunately, the reason the rabbit knew about people was that it already belonged to one when I found it and took it home. This was why my mother made me return it.

It was a strange situation, the situation in which I first found the rabbit. It was like magic, although it was magic draped in sadness. For everything in Grand Junction, Wyoming, was colored gray, gray the color of despair. Not even magic rabbits could escape this.

But anyhow, I was telling you about the strange situation in which I found the rabbit. I was out with my friend Kira, out walking. Kira and Lindsey were two of the few friends I had in my childhood. Kira lived down the street from my mother's second rental house after leaving my dad, the Ord Street house. Kira had three sisters and no brothers. One sister, Shana, was my sister Annie's age. Shana and Annie were friends like Kira and I. Maybe Kira and I were friends because we both knew about hopelessness. Kira had a mother, Alice, who was anorexic. Often, I would meet Alice on the street walking, walking, walking fast around the block. I didn't understand it then, but I guess she was trying to wear her body, and her pain, away. She usually had an apple with her. Recently, my mother told me that for a long time all Alice ate was that one apple, one apple each day. Alice's eating disorder finally caught her when she was in her forties and had let go of it. Through the eating disorder and then after, her heart hung on as long as it could, and then, it too let go, and she went with it.

Kira's father was Bill, and he was scary. Somehow I have a memory of him attacking one of Kira's sisters. I don't know if I really saw that. I'm not sure where the memory came from. But anyhow, I have this image, like a misplaced photograph from someone else's album, in my head. Her house, one block down from mine on Ord Street, was the heaviest place I had ever been. This is saying something, given my familiarity with heavy places.

So, as I was saying, Kira and I were out walking. We were walking along Grand Street, near the first house my mother rented, after she left my father. Somewhere along Grand Street we discovered the rabbit. Actually, there were more rabbits than one. This was part of the magic. There were bunches of rabbits. Running, hopping, grazing rabbits out in an empty, grassy lot right next to a little house surrounded by trees. This was the other part of the magic. These rabbits were free. And yet, unlike normal wild Wyoming rabbits, jackrabbits, or cottontails, these rabbits were hanging out together, and visible, in a large comfortable group. We could hardly believe our luck. Rabbits, lots and lots of rabbits, with all the wonderful traits rabbits have, out grazing in an empty lot just waiting for us to gather them up and take them home.

Kira and I spent what must have been hours chasing and chasing those rabbits, desperately trying to catch one. Finally, Kira gave up. It was getting late and she had to go home. I, however, was obsessed with those rabbits. I had to have one. Sometimes I still get that way, obsessed with the idea of a new puppy or kitten. Until the obsession passes, it is very hard for me to shake my thoughts away. I have to struggle to think of anything else. So, obsessed with the idea of bringing home one of those rabbits, I stayed in that lot long after Kira left. I stayed in that lot until I finally caught one.

It was after dark by the time I got home with that rabbit, tucked under my coat, hidden. I went straight to my room in the basement of our house, on the other side of my brother Martin's room. I went straight to my room without talking to anyone. My mother was still not home. When I got to my room, I hid the rabbit in my closet. I made a home for the rabbit there, intending to take it out to get air and sun during the afternoon hours when my mother was out, and I was done with school. Somehow, I knew my mother would not let me have that rabbit. I don't know how I knew. It did not occur to me that the rabbit might belong to someone, and thus, that I had stolen the little white rabbit. As far as I was concerned, the rabbit's appearance was one of those strange, inexplicable, yet wonderful, things that every once in awhile, just happens. One does not question such a thing. One does not think, how did this rabbit get here? Or, why a large group of rabbits free in an empty lot? I had only done what any reasonable person would do upon finding such a rabbit. I took the rabbit home.

What was odd about this was how little I recognized the oddness at the time. I don't mean that it was odd to catch and bring home the rabbit. That part made sense. The odd part was the hiding-of-the-rabbit in my closet. The odd part was the not-telling-my-mother. What I mean to say is that I was a child who never did anything wrong. I was perpetually worried about hurting my mother. And somehow, I felt that hurting my mother, whom I adored, was something I was always on the verge of doing. I did not have to do anything in particular to hurt my mother, just by being, there was this potential, this potential of hurting her. So I certainly did not want to actually, actively, do anything, anything bad, which would be sure to hurt her. That is why it was so strange that I hid the little rabbit from my mother, without thinking twice.

But odd as it was, it did not last long, the hiding-of-the-rabbit. That night, as my mother tucked me in bed, she heard a strange scuffling in the closet. And the rabbit was discovered.

The Second Rabbit: Clarke, Gram, and the Rabbit on the Road

Once I saw an otherwise unseen rabbit when I was driving with my Gram and her husband, my grandfather, Clarke. As I told you, when my grandfather was alive, he would do all of the long distance driving. My grandfather was a wild driver. He forgot to shut car doors, often driving off with them still open. He turned corners fast, and made the car stop and start so much I would be perpetually nauseous. He seemed oblivious to all creatures, both in and outside of the car. I actually do not know what he saw aside from, most of the time, the road. At least once, with me, he did not see a rabbit. Once on the highway—I think we were on our way to the Halley family reunion in Estes Park—he ran over a rabbit. I was in the back seat and I saw him hit it through the front window. Then, I felt its small body under the car, two quick thumps. I cried quietly so that no one would notice. And no one did, not even my grandmother.

The Third Rabbit: Gram and the Rabbits at Windsor Gardens

My other Gram, Gram Brennan, who along with being my grandmother was also the mother of my mother, had rabbits where she lived. They were not her rabbits. They just lived there, often unseen. Like the rabbits, my Gram Brennan also lived her life mostly unseen. Gram Brennan lived at Windsor Gardens. Windsor Gardens was a place to live when you were old, or if you were a small rabbit. Little girls did not live there. But my grandmother did.

Windsor Gardens was in Denver. Denver was the home of my mother when she was a little girl. Denver was the home of my mother's mother, my other grandmother. Like I told you, she lived in Windsor Gardens.

Windsor Gardens had rabbits running wild, small rabbits that belonged to no one. And there was a golf course. My grandmother played golf. And there were lots of buildings painted in pastel colors, buildings flowing in all directions, lots and lots of buildings. These buildings were not cramped together like in New York City. Nor were they in neat rows, like houses in a small town. They were casually placed in a variety of directions as though someone had tossed them, a big handful of buildings, across the endless lawn.

If you were a small girl, and I was, it was pretty easy to get lost in Windsor Gardens. When things around one look different, one can, with minimal confusion, find one's way. That's how it is in life. We know things because of what they are not. We know things because they are different from other things. At Windsor Gardens, everything was not different. Everything was the same. Everything was carefully, planfully the same. The buildings were the same, neat rectangles with two to four stories, in one of three or four mild, pastel colors. The lawn was the same, part of it was golf course, part of it was not. Yet all of it flowed on and on, trees and pastel buildings here and there, small walkways cutting patterns through the grass, leading nowhere in particular. Even the people were the same. That was the rule at Windsor Gardens. Everyone was white. No people of color at Windsor Gardens. Everyone was old, wrinkled, maybe slightly bent. Everyone had white hair. Everyone was rich with memories, memories maybe, or maybe not, remembered.

More than once, I would wander a bit too far from my grandmother's building. Then, in a rush of panic, I would realize that I had no idea where I was, or rather, I had no idea where my grandmother was in relation to me. I was somewhere, somewhere in the midst of Windsor Gardens. I was somewhere in the midst of sameness. Of course, it was no use asking if anyone knew where my grandmother lived. Lots of people at Windsor Gardens had that name, grandmother. The person asked could point me to an infinity of grandmothers. But I wanted my grandmother and only my grandmother. None other would do.

I am not sure how I found my way back those times. But, each time I got lost, I did, somehow, find my way back to my grandmother. At least that I know, for here I am telling you this story.

I used to spend hours chasing the rabbits at Windsor Gardens. They were little tiny, perpetually-baby rabbits. I don't know how those rabbits got to Windsor Gardens, or why they were so small. But there they were. Everywhere, small rabbits. Nobody got excited about seeing them, probably because nobody saw them. Except me. I, in contrast to the average Windsor Garden resident, always saw and always got excited about seeing rabbits. And if there was time, if my grandmother was not hurrying me somewhere or other, I would try and catch the rabbit. Once I cornered one, inside of a long row of car garages. It was the row right across from my grandmother's row, near her own personal car garage. I cornered the rabbit, poor frightened thing. Of course, I did not want to hurt that rabbit. I never, ever, would have hurt a rabbit. But this the rabbit did not know. I wanted to catch the rabbit and take it home with me, first back to my grandmother's and then back home to Grand Junction where I lived with my mother. But just when I finally had that rabbit cornered, an old man came to get something from his garage. What are you doing, he asked me. And the rabbit, smart rabbit, got away.

I did not love this grandmother, the grandmother who was my mother's mother, as much as my other grandmother. This grandmother was not magic like my other grandmother. But it was something else as well. This grandmother did not love me. Or, at least, she did not love me like my other grandmother did. With my other grandmother, I was special. I mattered. It is quite a thing to matter, to really matter, to someone. I mattered to my grandmother Clarke much like the rabbits mattered to me. She saw me.

I did not dislike my grandmother Brennan. And I doubt that she disliked me. I don't think she felt that strongly, one way or another, about anyone. I don't think she felt that strongly. Actually, I don't know if my grandmother felt at all. I think she had given up on feeling long before I met her. As a child, this made me mad. As a child, my grandmother's lovelessness made me mad. Although I would not have been able to put either her lack of feeling, or my anger, to words. The words had to wait until now.

And now, now, as always, it is too late. It is too late for understanding. My grandmother is too far away. Dead actually. Which is pretty far. And now, I am simply angry at the whole thing. It is like a long, cruel joke played on my grandmother. It is like a joke, played by no one in particular, that has been passed down and down through the generations of my family.

At one time, before she lived at Windsor Gardens surrounded by rabbits that she could not see, my Gram Brennan had a husband. She had a husband just like my other gram had Clarke. That man, Gram Brennan's husband, was my mother's father. That man would have been my grandfather, except that he died first. He was a doctor. But it didn't matter. It never does when it comes to dying. Even though he was a doctor, he died, suddenly, of cancer. He died, suddenly, while my mother was away. And she never got to say goodbye.

When the man who would have been my grandfather died, my mother was in her first year of college. She was at an all-women's college in San Francisco. For some reason, some reason we do not know, my grandmother wanted my mother to go to this college. My grandmother made all the arrangements, and sent my mother there. My grandmother was too passive, too numb, too silent, for wanting. My grandmother had long ago given up wanting, wanting anything, so we don't know why she wanted this, she wanted this for her youngest daughter. She wanted that her youngest daughter, who was to become my mother, go to this all-women's Catholic College in San Francisco. She wanted it. And she made it happen. We don't know why.

But then, my mother's father died. And there was no money. My mother's father had been, among other things, a gambler. Like most gamblers, sometimes he won, sometimes he lost, but mostly he lost. When he died, suddenly, of cancer, it was at a time when there was no money, not a time when there was. So because there was no money, my mother had to return home. She only stayed there one year at the college in San Francisco. And that year her father died. He died before I was even an idea. And I can tell you, that was a good thing. I never knew that man. And it's a good thing.

Gram Brennan had a crazy husband. He was crazy. And, often, he was drunk. And he did terrible things. They are too terrible to tell. And so, I won't. I will let those secrets rest, secrets still. They aren't my secrets anyhow.

But I will tell you this. More than once, my mother, still a child, still able to see, watched my grandmother be taken, on a stretcher, taken bleeding, taken from the house. I think my mother thought that she had died. She was only a little girl, my mother. My mother was only a little girl then. And she thought her mother had died. And it is amazing really that he did not kill her. He tried. But she lived in spite of him. This was before I was born. This was when my mother was a little girl. This was long ago, long before I came to be, a little girl, looking for rabbits.

My Grandmother and the Cleaning Lady

My other grandmother, the grandmother I adored, always had a cleaning lady. And she always had a clean house. Maybe the two were related, maybe not. There were many things my grandmother had. Cleanliness and objects, order and control, belonged to my grandmother like a birthright. And with my grandmother, I became a part of all that. I could breathe easy, finally, at least for a time.

As you know, when I was a child, I went to visit Gram for two weeks in the summer. I went every summer. It was a ritual. When I got to my grandmother's house, the first thing I would do was bring my things to her room and unpack them. She would make space for me in her closet. She gave me a drawer in her bureau. There was a place for me. I belonged.

When I visited my grandmother's house, I would stay with her in her room. She had her own room. A long time ago she used to share a room with my grandfather. But when I was still very small, she moved out. She wanted her own room. So, at the far end of the house, they fixed up a bedroom just for her. It was a big beautiful room, with a fireplace and windows overlooking the rose garden. It was filled with light. She had twin beds in her room, one of which was always mine. Next to her bed was the door to the dressing room. She had a dressing room with mirrors covering one wall, and a place to sit, to sit and look at yourself in the mirror. The dressing room had a walk-in closet that contained endless pairs of shoes and an enormous silver safe. My grandmother kept her jewelry in that safe. She had lots of jewelry, including a long pearl necklace that I loved. My grandmother said she would give me the pearl necklace when she died, but I didn't want to think about her dying. From the dressing room, you could also go into my grandmother's bathroom. This bathroom had two doors, one at either end. One door took you back into my grandmother's dressing room; the other went into my grandfather's bedroom.

I did not go into my grandfather's bedroom very often. Somehow I knew it was a place one should not go. It was everything my grandmother's room was not. My grandfather's bedroom was dark. It had a double bed and no view of the rose garden. It had no dressing room with mirrors, and no fireplace. It was a place for sleeping, not a place one went to think or read or spend their time. It was a man's room.

There were many rooms in that house. Above the basement, in the middle floor, my grandmother had made a room, a special room, just for my sister and me. My sister and I, being girls, were special. This was because we were the first girls that my grandmother had. We were the daughters of her first son, Simon. He was the first of her children to have children of his own. His first child, my grandmother's first grandchild, was a boy, my brother Martin. Then I was born, and being long awaited by my grandmother, they named me after her, Jean Halley. Then came my sister, Annie. She was named after my other grandmother, who was not so interested in girls, or grandchildren either, Fiona Anne O'Malley.

Anyhow, my grandmother whose house was on a hill made up a room especially for my sister Annie and me. It was called The Girls' Room, and it was blue. In this room, everything matched. The wallpaper matched the bedspreads, and these matched the carpet. Even the pillows wore cases of the same design as the flowers on the wall. And, along with the twin beds, nightstand, and reading lamps, the room even had a small mirror with a place to sit and look at yourself, just like my grandmother's dressing room. Sitting and looking at yourself was something girls were meant to do.

I was not very interested in the mirror. In many ways, I was not a very good Girl. This was probably a bit of a disappointment to my grandmother, but she never let on. My little sister, however, did like looking in the mirror. Maybe this was because she was unseen in my family. She was almost invisible. Maybe looking in the mirror was to make sure that someone saw her.

The thing I loved most about The Girls' Room was the two little cabinets, one for Annie and one for me, that my grandmother had attached to the wall. These cabinets were wooden, with glass fronts, and three shelves each. My grandmother filled them with little porcelain animals and dolls and things. I loved the animals especially.

I was mean to my sister about those cabinets. Periodically, I would change my mind about which cabinet was hers and which was mine. She had no say. This was probably true for my little sister in most areas of her life, not just with me, not just about the cabinets. Being the older sister, decisions such as cabinet allocation were up to me. The cruel thing was that just as she was getting attached to one or another object in her cabinet, I would decide it was actually my cabinet; her cherished object was actually mine.

For some reason, when I turned eight, I started being mean to my little sister, not just about the cabinets, but in general. I think it had to do with her being so small, so very vulnerable. She was even smaller than I, too small for the circumstances of our lives. I could not handle the fact of her smallness. Already, for me, the danger was too much. And so, I think this is why I was mean to her. She was too small. This is the hardest memory to remember. I was so mean to my little sister. I guess, really, the hardest thing about a memory one does not want to remember isn't the remembering. It is the unchangeability of it.

The odd thing about The Girls' Room was that I never stayed in it. Instead, when I went to visit my grandmother, she had me stay in her room with her. I loved to stay in my grandmother's room, with her sleeping in the bed right next to mine. And at any rate, I would have been scared to stay by myself, on the middle floor, in The Girls' Room. But I never told my grandmother that. I knew that to tell her of my fear would have been rude. I never even told her that I preferred, loved really, to stay with her. For, indicating any need, any personal desire, was considered Bad Manners. So, not knowing of my preference, maybe my grandmother simply enjoyed my company and this is why she had me stay with her. Or, maybe she realized it was dangerous, unsafe, to have me stay alone in The Girls' Room. I don't know. Like many things, this too remained unsaid.

When I visited my grandmother, we had a routine. Really, it was her routine and she shared it with me. It is a lovely thing to be wrapped up in, to disappear into someone else's routine. In the summer at my grandmother's, I felt surrounded by purpose. The days went, much too quickly, each with a border of sameness and a distinct touch of difference inside.

My grandmother was an early riser. I, on the other hand, have never been an early riser. This meant that I was never awake when my grandmother got out of bed at four thirty in the morning. It was inevitably a surprise to me, finding her bed empty when I woke around eight o'clock. I would look over at her place to sleep, where she had been the last time I looked before falling into sleep myself, and see that, once again, she had gotten up without me. Disappointed at that loss of time, time I could have been up with my grandmother, I would hurry out of bed and into the kitchen to find her. She got up in the morning to have tea, and make breakfast for my grandfather. Meals were always for someone else, particularly men and small children, whichever happened to be around, which included me. Whether or not my grandmother ate was not the point. She was the maker of meals. In fact, I do not remember my grandmother eating. She cooked, she served us, she sat, elegantly, with us, and looked on while we ate. But I have no visual memory of her taking food into her mouth, chewing, swallowing. Maybe in my grandmother's time, women did not eat. There were many things women did not do.

Of course, even this, even this seemingly solid thing of being female, even this depended on what kind of woman you were. My grandmother was one kind. My mother, when she left my father, became another. The differences were not merely matters of family, of blood or marriage. They involved a funny mix of money and morality and having men.

Money and morals often went together in my family. For men, it was simple. If they had one—money—it was understood that they had the other, but not vice versa. For men, it didn't really matter what they did. It was about what they had. For women, it was more complicated. They needed money and men to be legitimate, to be moral, to be good. Yet even for women, a lack of money alone was a suspicious sign, a sign of moral failings. My mother, of course, lost all her money and all her morality, when she left my father. Or really, according to my family, it was never her money to begin with. She could not be moral or clean or good without my father, and his money. Yet, the thing all the women shared, with or without money, with or without morals, was men's rage, even my grandmother, even her cleaning lady, even me.

But my grandmother, my grandmother was good. And she had money. And so, as a woman, a good and virtuous woman, my grandmother's day revolved around this meal making process. If we went out of the house to do something, shop or visit a relative, our event was bound by the making of meals. A number of phone calls had to happen, and preparations made in the kitchen, before we could leave. This was all mysterious to me, this schedule of my grandmother's. But it was the bedrock of her routine, a routine that had been set long ago, and was out of everyone's hands, including my grandmother's. So we followed the schedule, each meal when it was meant to be, and time passed. But making meals was not the only thing my grandmother did. She did other things too. She tended her roses. She read. She played cards with me, or on her own if I was not there. And, on a regular basis, she played bridge with my grandfather and people they knew. She went to Mass. She had a cocktail every afternoon at five o'clock with my grandfather. And they watched the evening news. She went grocery shopping.

Because everything with my grandmother was a good thing, a thing I wanted to do, I even loved going grocery shopping together. We would climb into her big and fancy car and she would back us slowly out of the driveway. The streets in Kidron were twisty. They curved and wound up and down the hill on which her house was built. The grocery store was below the hill, so we wound our way down with that big car's nose stretching out in front of us. My grandmother had to tell the car to turn long before the corners because the car was so big it needed time to prepare. When we arrived at the grocery store, my grandmother would pull slowly up and park, and we would climb out of the car.

In the store, my grandmother would let me push the cart. And she would tell me to pick out my favorite vegetable for dinner. I loved corn, but also mashed potatoes. She would get them both. She would always ask if there was anything in particular I had been wanting. There always was. I adored sweets. But knowing it was rude to ask for things, I would tell my grandmother there was nothing in particular. Somehow, in spite of my polite denial, she knew and would pick out something sweet. And, as we wove our way through the aisles, we would discuss things.

This was the best part about being with my grandmother. She listened to me. I would tell her things. And I was heard.

I told my grandmother about my friends, or friends I did not have. I told her what I thought about things. I had things to say. My grandmother told me things too. Sometimes she told me about her family, which was my family as well. She told me about our history, because it was important that I knew. She told me news about my cousins; what was happening with Uncle Mat and Aunt Kristen in Denver, how Davey did in school, that Aunt Amanda's father had visited two weeks before. Once she told me that her cleaning lady had done a bad thing. My grandmother always had a cleaning lady.

Because the cleaning lady needed to clean someone else's home for money, she was another kind of woman. It did not matter who she was. It was what she was. For a long time, all the while my father was growing up and well into my own childhood, Mrs. Mueller was the cleaning lady. Mrs. Mueller, everyone said, was a part of the family. But still she did not eat with us at family meals. She just did the dishes. Mrs. Mueller was old and German and had a sick husband. He spent his days at home on the couch, in their dark living room, in their small house. And, one thing I knew somehow, although no one ever really told me, Mrs. Mueller's husband did bad things to her. She was scared of him.

But finally Mrs. Mueller's husband died. It was a blessing in disguise my grandmother said. Even so, it meant that Mrs. Mueller moved away. She moved to California to live with her son and his family. Being an old woman and alone, without much money, she could not stay in Kidron. So even though she was a part of the family, we never saw her again.

Mrs. Mueller was not the cleaning lady who did a bad thing. That cleaning lady was just a cleaning lady, not a part of the family like Mrs. Mueller. But still my grandmother liked her. My grandmother told me she was a good cleaning lady. Given this, my grandmother was very surprised when she did the bad thing. I will tell you what she did. She chopped up her husband and put him under the bed.

And then, she did not tell anyone. This part made sense to me. How was she to explain this, and who would she tell anyhow? But in spite of her silence, they found out. She lived in a trailer court in Kidron, she, her chopped-up husband, and their two children. Well, eventually her husband began to smell. Then he smelled even worse. Finally, the neighbors could not stand the stench any longer. They called and complained to the police. And so, the cleaning lady was found out. I asked my grandmother if she was going be the cleaning lady still. And my grandmother told me she couldn't. This was a real problem, as finding a good cleaning lady was hard in Kidron.

After Mrs. Mueller left, there was a series of cleaning ladies. The cleaning lady with the chopped-up husband was only one of many. I never got to know any of the cleaning ladies after Mrs. Mueller. They came and went too fast. In contrast, everyone in the family knew Mrs. Mueller. She had watched my father grow up, and all my uncles too. And she knew just how things should be around the house. I remember that she worried particularly about my grandmother's silver.

My grandmother had a lot of silver. We used it for special occasions, like when all the family came over for a meal. After the meal, Mrs. Mueller would do the dishes. I liked to help. Somehow I came to know that Mrs. Mueller did not really want my help, but she pretended she did to please my grandmother. In this, Mrs. Mueller was like me. We both wanted to please my grandmother.

When it came to washing the silver, Mrs. Mueller was pretty fussy. It had to be washed by hand, not in the dishwasher. This was okay with me. We did not have a dishwasher at my house, where I lived with my mother. Dishwashers, among other things my grandmother had and my mother did not, were too expensive. Maybe out of loyalty to my mother, I did not like using the dishwasher. So we washed the silver by hand, which was just regular washing to me. Immediately after washing, each piece of silver had to be carefully dried, wrapped and put away. Mrs. Mueller was very worried about the silver getting spots due to a poor washing job. Inevitably, my washing was a poor washing job. Mrs. Mueller stopped letting me wash the silver.

Even though she was a part of the family, I did not spend much time with Mrs. Mueller, just she and I. I did not spend much time with my uncles or my grandfather either. But that was different. They were men. It was against the rules for girls or women to spend time alone with men, even if they were in the family. Once, however, Mrs. Mueller took me, by myself, to see her house. Actually, she was probably caring for me and needed to get something at her house, so she brought me along, not wanting to leave me alone. But at the time, the way I understood it, Mrs. Mueller was taking me on a special visit to her home.

We went, Mrs. Mueller and I, in her car. It was a small white car. It was very old, and not at all like my grandmother's car. Because

Kidron was such a little town, Mrs. Mueller didn't live far from my grandmother's place. But it seemed far. I had never been to that part of town. In Mrs. Mueller's neighborhood there were no trees. This made the sky particularly big, and the houses even smaller. I already wanted to go home to my grandmother's.

Mrs. Mueller's house was a dirty white color, just like her car. I followed her inside. Mrs. Mueller did not show me the whole house. Instead she left me in the kitchen while she hurried off to get something. Next to the kitchen was the living room where Mrs. Mueller's husband lay on the couch, in the dark. All the blinds on the windows were down. I think he might have been watching the television. And I don't think he wanted to meet me. Mrs. Mueller did not introduce me. This was unusual. In Kidron, I was used to being considered special. I was always introduced. And I was greeted everywhere I went.

Waiting there for Mrs. Mueller, I was scared. Mrs. Mueller was gone for what seemed like a very long time, such a long time that I began to feel angry at Mrs. Mueller for leaving me there next to her scary sick husband on the couch. Yet, what I remember most clearly is that Mrs. Mueller seemed scared too. Mrs. Mueller seemed scared in her own house. Eventually, however, Mrs. Mueller did come to retrieve me from my waiting in the kitchen. Then she hurried us both out of the house and back to the car.

I have a funny memory of us in her living room, rushing to the front door, rushing by her husband. With the memory I have a sense of myself knowing that this cannot be true. Or maybe the disbelief has been added to the memory since then. Or, maybe, the disbelief was always there, it is the memory that has been added. I cannot know for certain what was real—the feeling or the image. With my childhood nothing was certain, even as it happened.

But let me tell you the memory. I remember that as we rushed by him lying there on the couch, Mrs. Mueller's husband reached out to grab her. Somehow I knew he was not reaching out to grab her gently, to touch her, kiss her, tell her good-bye. Somehow I knew he really wanted to hurt Mrs. Mueller, to hurt her badly. Mrs. Mueller quickly sidestepped his reaching arm. We made it to the door and out. Rage followed us, rushing, rushing to the car.

Chapter 6

The Lives of Cows

In this chapter, I investigate the production and reproduction of biopower through the lives of cows, past and present, in terms of the food they eat, and where and how they live. Biopower involves the management of life and its reproduction. Modern meat production concerns the management of animal life and the ongoing reproduction of animals as capital. Most modern American beef cattle spend over half of their short lives barely alive. They are obese, eating foods that cows did not evolve to eat, such as corn and other animals. They are kept alive by constant monitoring, veterinarian care, and the use of antibiotics as they balloon into fatter and fatter beasts. Then at a very young 14 to 16 months, enormous and sick, the animals are slaughtered and processed for meat. Cows' very lives have mimicked the processes of industrialization. Their bodies have grown bigger and bigger as their lifespan has become shorter and shorter. Contemporary cow death, cow transformation from animal to meat, has become quicker and quicker. Industrialization has meant more cow, faster.

Grass, Corn, and Cows

Understanding the lives of cows requires understanding the shifting nature of land in the United States. In the late nineteenth century, US land prices went up markedly as the available grassland receded. There was less grassland due to the exponential increase in non-Native humans—homesteaders—living on more and more of the land. The railroads hastened the arrival of homesteaders; as the reach of the railroads spread, so did the non-Native humans' ability to live on more of the western land, hitherto inhabited primarily by Native Americans. Because of overstocking the grassland with cattle, the land became less and less fertile. As land became more expensive, and the available, productive grassland contracted, the meat industry focused on other ways to produce beef fast through cows that grew bigger, more quickly, and with less grass. They increasingly raised and fattened cows on grains, and as the animals grew fatter, faster, the meat industry slaughtered their cattle younger and younger.

As discussed in chapter 2, earlier cows lived more years and ate mostly grass. These past cows had five or six years grazing before being sold and slaughtered. While they did eat some grain, their humans mostly allowed them to do what cows evolved to do—graze on grass. By the middle of the twentieth century, cows still grazed most of each year on grasslands, but only lived for two or three years. By World War II, "animals were rarely kept on the range beyond 1–2 years."[1] They spent the rest of their short lives being fattened on grain in feedlots. Today modern meat industry cows only live around 14 to 16 months, and spend only the first six or so of those eating grass.[2]

In part, it was shrinking grasslands that led to the increase of corn in the lives of cows. Yet, conversely, the growing *abundance* of corn also played a role in its developing importance as cattle feed, and with cattle feed came feedlots. Of course, cows cannot just eat corn out in the wild. They do not graze on corn. Having no opposable thumbs (or machines taking on the job of thumbs), it is pretty tough for cows to get the corn kernels off of the cob; cows eat corn fed to them by humans. Rather than eating corn once in a day otherwise spent in a field grazing, in the mid-twentieth century, people made feeding corn to cows an intensive period of cow life. Cows began to spend a period of several months eating corn and more (and more) corn. Ross notes, "While cheap grassland continued to be a cornerstone of beef production, corn began increasingly to influence the price of beef as the burden of productivity shifted to feed lots which, in turn, 'developed as part of a system to market feed grains,' in particular, the corn surplus."[3]

In other words, with more corn than anyone knew what to do with, people opted to feed it to cows and other livestock as a way to fatten them faster. And as corn became central to the feeding and fattening of cows, the meat industry instituted a normalized or expected grain feeding stage in the lives of beef cattle—in feedlots. Instead of lives lived from birth to slaughter grazing grass as evolution demanded possibly with some grain supplement, cattle began to be (and continue to be) fattened in a period of intensive binging on grain for a number of months before their transformation into processed meat. This period happens at a feedlot, a place set up to support cows' standing still (often deep in their own manure) binging on corn for months.

Cow-Calf Operations

At birth, today's beef cows spend about six months with their mothers nursing and grazing on grass. This first stage in the lives of meat cows is the beef industry's "cow-calf operations." The modern industrialization of meat impacted this stage the least of all. In cow-calf operations, cattle ranchers breed their own brood cows to produce beef industry calves. From conception, these babies are meant for someone's plate.

Cow-calf operations have historically been, and usually still are, distinct from the next stage in the lives of US beef industry cows, "feedlots." After raising them for about six months, the cow-calf operations complete their part of meat production and sell their calves to the feedlots for fattening. The cattle ranchers who run cow-calf operations do not normally own and run feedlots. The beef industry is less consolidated than the pork and chicken industries. Whereas pigs and chicken now largely spend their lives confined to a single facility (and never spend time outside or in the sun), beef cattle are born on hundreds of thousands of independent ranches across the western states and then sent to slaughterhouses owned by the big four meatpacking companies (Cargill subsidiary Excel, ConAgra/Swift and Company, Farmland National Beef, and Tyson subsidiary IBP). The meatpackers, rather than the ranchers, enjoy the lucrative end of the business. These enormous conglomerates slaughter over 80 percent of the cattle in the United States, but they rely on the smaller, independent operations to handle the land-intensive aspect of ranching.[4]

When I visited my grandparents for two weeks in the summer, we had an evening ritual. Not every evening, but often, my grandfather would drive my grandmother and me around his properties so that we could check up on things. We drove for miles on winding country roads, some dirt, some paved. We drove past my grandfather's farms, where corn was grown and wheat. We drove past his cattle. Part of his small empire included a cow-calf operation that we visited.

My grandmother sat in the front seat next to my grandfather. I sat in the back. We all looked out the window as we drove, mostly in silence. Sometimes my grandfather would point this or that out. The corn looked good. The cows looked healthy. One year driving past a pasture of cows grazing with their one-month-old-or-so babies, perhaps to amuse himself, my grandfather "gave" me a calf. We drove into the pasture so that I could see her up close from the car. She was small and red with white markings on her face. She had tiny hooves and a small swooshing tail. She looked just like her mother, in miniature. I only saw "my calf" that one time. Yet I thought of her for months, wondering where she was, what she was doing. I even thought of a brand for her, a brand that would be mine alone. It involved the initials of my name merged together into one small and connected design.

Always naive and ridiculously trusting (oddly, a characteristic that comes with trauma according to some scholars), only years later did I finally realize what happened to "my calf." Around the same time, as a young adult, I also realized what had happened to my childhood Shetland pony. A decade before, I had outgrown her. You do not have to be very big to outgrow a Shetland pony. When I grew too tall and too heavy for her to carry me, she was already quite old. I had been told she had been put out to pasture near where we lived in Grand Junction, retired to a life of leisure pony-style. Strangely, that same year on one of my childhood visits to my grandparents, I saw her in one of the pens at my grandfather's salebarn and could not understand why she was there.

It turns out that, until 2007 when Congress effectively banned the slaughter of horses in United States slaughterhouses, a large number of old, no-longer-useful-to-their-humans horses and ponies ended their lives with cows and other livestock at slaughterhouses. In the United States, humans eating cows is normative, eating horses is not. Our dogs and cats, however, have commonly eaten horseflesh. And the meat was also shipped to Europe and other places where people eat horse.

Politeness and gender prohibited my asking questions of my grandfather about the calf, or my little pony. I did not understand, but accepted fully, the mystery of male power.

Cattle ranchers handle the risky component of the contemporary meat industry, and for relatively little pay-off. Indeed, because of economic problems, my father and his family were among about 500,000 who left the cattle business in the final decades of the twentieth century, leaving only 800,000 US cattle ranchers. And those still struggle to survive. Journalist Eric Schlosser writes, "Without receiving a fraction of the public attention given to the northwestern spotted owl, America's independent cattlemen have truly become an endangered species." Schlosser explains,

> Ranchers currently face a host of economic problems: rising land prices, stagnant beef prices, oversupplies of cattle, increased shipments of live cattle from Canada and Mexico, development pressures, inheritance

> taxes, health scares about beef. On top of all that, the growth of the fast food chains has encouraged consolidations in the meatpacking industry. McDonald's is the nation's largest purchaser of beef. In 1968 McDonald's bought ground beef from 175 local suppliers. A few years later, seeking to achieve greater product uniformity as it expanded, McDonald's reduced the number of beef suppliers to five.[5]

As early as 1964, ranching authority Harold Oppenheimer found it necessary to "dispel the fiction of the millionaire rancher who made it on operations." Rather than profit, ranchers in the calf-cow business very often experience losses.[6] Over time, finances for US ranches have only grown worse. One rancher told Pollan that from one generation to the next in the business, his father made more money on 250 cattle than he does on 850.[7]

Another time, the only time I remember checking up on my grandfather's cattle with my uncles, we rode in my grandfather's large jeep. When we went driving with my grandmother, we never went in the jeep. Ladies do not ride in jeeps. I, a mere girl, could still go in the jeep. I sat in the backseat with my uncles, Nat and Bart. The five sons eventually inherited my grandfather's business, including the cow-calf operation, after he died and I was an adult. I was told that he set aside a small amount of it all, five million dollars or so, for my grandmother, to keep her comfortable. The rest, the majority, went to his five sons. Eventually, as I said, they sold off the cattle business. It was no longer lucrative. Yet then, that day in the jeep with my uncles, we still owned cattle and we were checking up on some of them.

We drove cross country into a pasture where a huge black bull was breeding cows for the cow-calf operation. My uncle Bart, as the youngest male, had to jump out to open the barbed wire gate. We drove into the pasture and my uncle shut the gate fast and ran after us. As a joke, my grandfather drove off, toward the cattle, leaving my uncle running behind. The bull spotted us and, being feisty and aggressive, snorted, put his huge head down to charge and started running at my uncle. My grandfather laughed and continued driving away from my frantic uncle trying to catch up with and jump in the jeep. Just before the bull reached him, my grandfather stopped the jeep and let my uncle quickly open the door and leap in. Instead of bashing into my uncle, the powerful bull rammed the jeep, lifting it off the ground a bit and leaving a small dent where his head made contact.

Feedlots

After six months of living as cows evolved to live, meat industry cattle spend another 60 to 150 days at feedlots. Writing about beef production for a scientific journal in 1977, G. M. Ward, P. L. Knox, and B. W. Hobson note,

> The feedlot developed as a part of a system to market feed grains. The feed grains (for livestock) usually refer to corn, sorghum, and barley . . . In times when the major grain market was livestock feed, it became profitable to use large amounts of grain to speed up the growth and fattening process which resulted in beef that was uniformly tender, juicy, and generally very acceptable to consumers.[8]

The United States Department of Agriculture (USDA) supported the corn-producers by developing a grading system that prioritized the meat of corn-fed cows. Congress created the United States Agricultural Products Inspection and Grading Act in 1924. The act sanctioned the grading of livestock and meat by the federal government.[9] This system ranked "marbled meat," meat that has intramuscular fat, as "choice" meat. Corn-fed cows more rapidly add marbled meat than do grass-fed cows. Ward, Knox, and Hobson write, "Because of the more favorable price, the choice grade is the predominant goal of feeders, and thus it is apparent that the existing grading system has imposed a structure on the industry which in turn has institutionalized consumer tastes and a demand for grain-fed cattle."[10]

Corn-fed beef also looks different than grass-fed. When we buy meat in the supermarket we are used to seeing (and eating) meat that was raised on corn. Since most consumers buy "choice" corn-fed beef, this is what they have come to expect and desire. And this perpetuates the cycle.

The appearance and taste of beef from corn-fed cows is not fundamentally or "naturally" better than that from grass-fed cows. Further, studies show that eating corn-fed meat has more health risks than eating grass-fed. Instead of actually being better meat in some value-neutral way, Ross notes that "the economic interests of corn-producers and persistent pressure to dispose of grain surpluses" played a central role in conditioning the consumer preference for corn-fed meat.[11]

Aside from the issue of taste, there are many reasons to argue that grass-fed beef is better than corn-fed. For one, grass-fed cows are healthier cows. They are eating the food that they evolved to eat naturally as ruminants— grass. As their bodies were made to consume grass, grass-fed cows stay healthier and need significantly less medical care—including significantly less medicines—than corn-fed cows. This means the humans who eat them also eat less medicine (medicine that the human eaters do not need).

As most of the animals living at the feedlot are sick to some extent, they need near-constant medical care. Pollan writes, "The species is evolving, in other words, to help absorb the excess biomass coming off America's cornfields. But the cow's not there quite yet, and a great many feedlot cattle— virtually all of them to one degree or another, according to several animal scientists I talked to—are simply sick."[12] Instead of being something used for extraordinary circumstances, as with a periodically ill animal, medical care is used almost continuously, with almost all meat industry cows, as part of the everyday means to keep the animal alive until he or she is big enough to merit slaughter. It helps that we have shortened their life span significantly. Pollan notes that beef cattle "rarely live on feedlot diets for more than 150 days, which might be about as long as their systems can tolerate."[13]

Medical care for beef cattle primarily involves antibiotics. Pollan notes, "What keeps a feedlot animal healthy—or healthy enough—are antibiotics. Rumensin inhibits gas production in the rumen, helping to prevent bloat; tylosin reduces the incidence of liver infection. Most of the antibiotics sold in America end up in animal feed—a practice that, it is now generally acknowledged, leads directly to the evolution of new antibiotic-resistant 'superbugs.'"[14] So, to top it all off, for the feedlots to do well, humans in power have to be willing to allow the feedlots to feed so many antibiotics to their animals that the antibiotics might not work when humans need them.

Public health advocates do not dispute giving antibiotics to animals that are ill. Rather, they worry that the drugs will no longer work on humans when the drugs are overused on animals. This happens when healthy animals are regularly fed antibiotic medicine to encourage their growth. However, Pollan explains, "the use of antibiotics in feedlot cattle confounds this distinction," that is, between using the drugs on sick animals and overusing them on healthy animals. Commonly on factory farms, or as discussed in chapter 1, concentrated animal feeding operations (CAFOs), "the drugs are plainly being used to treat sick animals, yet the animals probably wouldn't be sick if not for the diet of grain we feed them."[15]

The staff veterinarian at the Garden City, Kansas, feedyard Pollan visited, put this succinctly. "'They're made to eat forage,' Dr. Metzin explained, 'and we're making them eat grain ... It's not that they can't adjust.'" Indeed he continues, "'now we're breeding cattle to do well in a feedyard.'"[16]

"Doing well" in a feedlot means, simply, getting very fat, very fast, and at the lowest possible cost to the feedlot owners. Success in this venture has come to mean enormous US cows. Grain plays an important role in growing big cows, and growth hormones do too. Schlosser explains that growth hormones mean bigger cows, yet they also mean that "most American beef cannot be exported to the European Union, where the use of bovine growth hormones has been banned."[17]

Along with fat cows, "doing well" post-feedlot entails people wanting to purchase and eat the meat from the feedlot. For the industry to be successful—make a hearty profit—people have to want to consume lots and lots of cow meat, cow meat that grew fat on an unnatural food, that is, food that cows did not evolve to eat. People have to desire meat high in unsaturated fats. People have to be more than willing to consume meat that stood knee deep in feces for months, feces potentially containing "more than forty diseases that can be transferred to humans." (And this happens when cows carry some of the feces into the slaughterhouse and it moves inadvertently from the outside to the inside of the animal while she is processed into food for humans.) Cows did not evolve to live, for months, standing in their own waste.

In the interest of fat cows fast, we humans have selectively bred our beef cattle to "adjust" as Dr. Metzin puts it. We have and continue to breed our cows to eat a lot of corn, turn that corn into meat, grow fat, and do this without dying before it is time to be slaughtered. The project is still touch and go.

Biopolitics leads to this way of producing meat. In this, we allow the meat industry to treat the animals as it does, to produce meat in the profoundly unhealthy way that it does, to deeply damage the environment as it does. Further, in our biopolitical world we buy and eat this meat, meat that has been shown to be—in a variety of ways—harmful to us.

Nonetheless, in a certain light, the project is enormously successful. Today in the United States, we kill, buy, and eat meat in staggering quantities. Environmental writer, Imhoff illuminates, "In the United States alone, nearly 10 billion domesticated livestock—mostly chicken, pigs and cows—are raised and slaughtered annually . . . This is twice the number that America raised in 1980 and ten times more than in 1940."[18] For example, in terms of cows alone, according to the USDA, in 2006 the meat industry slaughtered almost 34 million cows. That same year, Americans consumed 28 billion pounds of beef.[19]

Chapter 7

Slaughterhouses and the Death of a Cow

If the meat industry offers a quintessential example of the development of the US economy, as argues Skaggs,[1] cows' lives offer a quintessential example of the growth of biopower in the lives of nonhuman animals.[2] They are pressed directly into the service of capital, as their bodies become meat.[3] Brutal, dangerous, and largely hidden from public view, the slaughterhouses—the owners, not the workers—make most of the money in beef. Ranchers and cowboys, who ironically take up a lot of space in our popular imagination, often barely make ends meet.

Slaughterhouses present one of the most dangerous work environments for American workers, and of course for cows. Some of that danger springs from the demand for killing cows fast, fast, fast. In a typical slaughterhouse, we have the capacity to kill hundreds and hundreds of cows each day. Too often, under extreme pressure to move too fast, workers process, bleed, and skin live cows as they transform the beasts into meat. One can only imagine the pain for the cows. For the underpaid, overworked meatpackers it takes little imagination to understand that this practice is extremely unsafe. Imagine dozens of humans with sharp knives, working quickly to skin and dissect enormous animals that are at times alive, conscious, and fighting.

As much as trauma bled through my childhood, and grips the lives of cows, trauma also shapes the experiences of slaughterhouse workers. They witness and take part in regular violence, violence beyond the violence of the actual kill, due to the speed and pressure the work entails. Skinning an animal alive is more than dangerous, it impinges upon, it traumatizes not only the animal but all those involved.

I want to place the slaughter of cows in the broader context of violence in US culture. Limerick describes how, in mainstream US thought, Americans believe themselves to have become a uniquely American people through the conquest of the frontier.[4] Like the popular ideas about masculinity as something born out of the subjugation of others, in popular thought, mainstream white Americans' Americanness springs from violence, from conquest of the other—Native people, animals, and the land.

Whereas violence makes America, violence is also increasingly understood as repugnant in normative civilized culture. Pachirat, drawing on the work of Norbert Elias, argues that the historical process in western industrialized nations of becoming "civilized" is a process where normative culture became increasingly antagonized and repelled by violence.[5] Herein lies a central contradiction in normative thought.

With Limerick, I argue that the thinking underlying normative US culture is that American people *became* through violence. As discussed in chapter 2, "we"—and again, a lot of people are left out of that we—underwent a transformation from what we were to *being American* through violent engagement with the "uncivilized." Further, men, "real men," continue to become men through sexual and other violence. Gender *happens* through this violence. Simultaneous to this ideology of becoming-through-violence, violence is also increasingly understood to be repulsive, and is therefore hidden from mainstream view. Whereas many in the United States celebrated the "necessary" violence of the war on Iraq as a show of manly, American power, and many believe in the "right" to own guns, most have not witnessed actual violence on bodies at war or the impact of the use of guns on humans or other animals. In the contemporary United States, most people eat meat but most have never taken part in, or even witnessed, the slaughter of an animal. In contrast to this, most people in the preindustrial United States used the guns they owned on animal bodies, nonhuman if not human, and ate the meat of animals that they themselves killed.

Pachirat reveals that violence today often happens in a "'zone of confinement,' a 'segregated and isolate territory,' in the words of sociologist Zygmunt Bauman, 'invisible' and 'on the whole inaccessible to ordinary members of society.'"[6] Pachirat notes:

> Close attention to how the work of industrialized killing is performed might thus illuminate not only how the realities of industrialized animal slaughter are made tolerable but the ways distance and

> concealment operate in analogous social processes: war executed by volunteer armies; the subcontracting of organized terror to mercenaries; and the violence underlying the manufacture of thousands of items and components we make contact with in our everyday lives. Such scrutiny makes it possible, as social theorist Pierre Bordieu puts it, "to think in a completely astonished and disconcerted way about things [we] thought [we] had always understood."[7]

Further, I argue that domestic violence such as the hidden, gendered, and sexual violence of incest transforms the home into another such simultaneously common and hidden zone of confinement. In this concealed space, gender is produced and reproduced.

In slaughterhouses, via violent transformation, not only meat but also race is produced.[8] In the United States, men of color, many undocumented, perform the dangerous labor of slaughter. Slaughter is dangerous not only for the cows. "The emphasis on speed in the new slaughterhouses—profits are measured by the quantity of processed meat per hour—translates into a rate of injury to workers that surpasses that of any other industry."[9] The working conditions are so bad that for the first time the New York City based Human Rights Watch, an organization that monitors human rights violations globally, reported on this single US industry. The 2005 report stated, "Packinghouse workers ... regularly suffer life-threatening on-the-job dangers with little training or adequate equipment, are discouraged by companies from reporting their injuries and are pressured not to join unions." As so many of the workers are immigrants, many undocumented, the workforce is often "either unaware of its rights because of language difficulties or fretful about speaking out and being deported."[10] The report noted that dangerous working conditions cost less for the slaughterhouse owners, "and the government does next to nothing."[11]

I follow Pachirat in examining "zones of confinement" where everyday and repugnant violence plays a role in the reproduction of day-to-day life; through violence the cows become meat, through eating meat, humans reproduce themselves. In a very basic sense, the cows, in their lives and in their deaths, deaths segregated from most humans' lives and hidden inside industrialized slaughterhouses, reproduce humans. The equally hidden, often sexual violence against girls—violence that happens in private domestic spaces, segregated from public view—reproduces traumatized and gendered human subjectivity.

My grandfather owned a salebarn in Wyoming, so he was a conduit from the people raising the cows to the people slaughtering the cows. He also raised cows himself, so he made money through selling his own cattle as well as through the auctioning of other ranchers' cattle. My grandfather's salebarn was the largest one west of the Mississippi, my father used to tell me proudly.

As a child I walked above cow on raised wooden pathways at my grandfather's salebarn. The raised pathways webbed around the pens filled with cattle and allowed humans to walk among and see the cows without touching them, without getting covered in muck, and without frightening them. Those pathways seemed like sidewalks for magical giants from the world of Jack and the beanstalk. They afforded a bird's eye view. And I can tell you, having walked them, that it's a pretty good view. I looked down on these enormous pens filled with manure and mud and animals. Your senses are assaulted when you are around cows crowded together at a salebarn. You don't just see them. You hear them, mooing and bellowing loudly. You feel the heat of their tightly packed-together dirty, muddy bodies. You taste the dust and straw kicked up into the air that makes your eyes itch. You smell cow.

Indeed, perhaps the most dramatic experience of being with cows is their smell. They have a very strong and particular odor—like wet dog or freshly cut grass—that is distinctly and definitively cow. Of course, like humans, the cows' odor changes depending on what you feed them. And we feed them not what's best for them—grass—but what makes them grow fat, fast—grain.

Cattle raised in huge numbers for beef are not like family pets. They have no names and they know no human well, so they are quite wary of human contact. Because they do not live at the salebarn, the cows I walked above looked anxious in their new surroundings.

The people who walked about on those raised pathways, the men (and in my childhood it was only men working at the salebarn), looked very much alike in their mud-and-manure-covered uniform of jeans, cowboy boots and hats, t-shirts in the summer, flannel and jackets in the winter. The only difference I could see was that some men were brown and some were white. Looking back, I now know that if they were Mexican American, they did the dirtier, more dangerous work and had more actual contact with cows. My grandfather was an avid racist and likely a member of the local Ku Klux Klan. He was also a good businessman: racism made good business sense. My grandfather worked to make and keep Mexican labor cheap. Racism afforded him an explanation for his exploitation.

The white men did the work that was a step or two removed from the bodies and feces and hooves of cows. I remember that the brown men avoided my eye contact and the white men knew my name. Although some might take a moment to greet me, most went about their business as though I was not there. It was clear that the cows were not the only ones in unfamiliar territory. Little girls had no place at the salebarn either.

Killing Cows

In the US beef industry, some people breed and raise the cows, some fatten them, others slaughter them and pack their meat to be sold, and then at the final stage, there are those who buy and eat their flesh. The slaughterhouses are merely a stage in the life and death of meat, yet the slaughterhouses monopolize the money to be made from the beef industry. Despite the fact that we focus most of our popular culture's attention on the ranchers—the Wild West, the cowboys, and the "pioneer spirit"—the heart of the moneymaking is the place where the cattle hearts stop beating, not where they begin.

Skaggs writes that the process is like an hourglass, with many people raising cows (the ranchers in cow-calf operations) and many people eating cows (the consumers) but, in the middle, not many making a killing on killing cows. In other words, at the waist of the hourglass, a small group has made and continues to make an immense amount of money off of the backs of cows—literally—and off of the ranchers.[12] As noted earlier, four giant competitors—Excel (owned by Cargill), ConAgra/Swift and Company, Farmland National Beef, and IBP—dominate the beef industry, controlling over 85 percent of the US market.[13] Moreover, by the end of the twentieth century, author and animal rights activist, Gail A. Eisnitz writes, "lax enforcement of antitrust laws during the Reagan and Bush administrations ... allowed [for] a consolidation of meatpacking power to levels higher than at any time in history, and a corresponding deregulation of slaughterhouse procedures."[14] Further, Eisnitz notes,

> According to the USDA, between 1984 and 1994, a few large, high-speed slaughter operations had driven roughly 2,000 small to mid-sized packers out of business—one-third of all packers in the United States. They also reduced the workforce while cranking up the killing speeds. Fewer employees were slaughtering more animals ... According to the USDA, in 1980, it took the country's 50 largest beef packing companies and 103 individual plants to slaughter three-quarters of the nation's cattle. By 1992, three firms were already slaughtering that percentage of animals in 29 plants.[15]

To survive as a profitable business, ranchers and feedlot owners who supply the cows to the four most powerful meatpacking companies must produce as much of their product—cow-to-be-meat—with as little lost labor or other resources in as short a time as is possible. The biopolitical management of life dictates that the bigger the cow, and the faster growing the cow, the better.

This has a number of implications for the cows. As discussed in chapter 6, they are fed lots of junk food—food that makes them fat fast, to the point of obesity. These increasingly unhealthy cows require hearty and regular doses of antibiotics to keep them alive, antibiotics that end up being passed on to the rest of us who eat cow. Then ironically, after so much effort spent to keep these obese beings alive—indeed because the cows rapidly balloon into larger and larger animals—their lives are cut short while still young. When it comes time to be slaughtered, cows are either sold from their most recent owners—the people who own the feedlot—or the slaughterhouse itself is fattening the cows before slaughter.

Somewhere around 14 to 16 months old, fattened (obese, really) cows are loaded into cattle trailers and carried to their last stop, the slaughterhouses. They used to walk for miles, for days, even months to the place of their slaughter. The distance they walked decreased significantly over the past two hundred years as transportation improved. Also, the invention of refrigerators made it possible to preserve dead cow longer, relieving live cows of significant time and travel.

Cows still walk to the site of their death; it's just a shorter walk. A law requires that the animals do so. The cows need to be at a certain standard of health before the federal government allows them to be slaughtered. This is not, of course, meant to benefit the cow. The USDA devised this test to be sure the cow is healthy before transforming its flesh into food. A cow that cannot walk, a "downed cow," could be a sick cow whose flesh is unfit for human consumption.

Given a tight profit margin, those in the beef industry want to make sure that there is little to no loss; this means that industry workers work to make each and every cow—well or not—walk to its own slaughter. And this is pretty tough on a downed cow. The Humane Society of the United States offers video footage at their website from numerous undercover investigations. Among their investigations, in 2008, the Humane Society looked into the sale and slaughter of dairy cows that were no longer producing enough milk to make them profitable.[16] Typically dairy farmers sell unproductive cows for slaughter.

The undercover investigators need to gain access to slaughterhouses, and can sometimes accomplish this by applying to work there. In their dairy cow investigation, the Humane Society undercover workers witnessed extensive abuse of dairy cows, videotaping this abuse with small cameras hidden in their clothing.

The Humane Society inspected numerous auctions and slaughterhouses. They found that dairy cows that were too frail or too ill to walk were ignored while they suffered for hours. In the end, potential profit carries more weight than the law that the animals must walk. The undercover investigators observed—and we can see it in their video footage—downed animals being beaten until they drag themselves on broken limbs to their own death. Machines drag animals, seemingly too sick to move on their own. Workers kick, beat, and shock other animals as they attempt to force the animals to stand up. One worker repeatedly and forcefully probes a downed cow in her eye. After beating another downed cow to no avail, a worker tries to force her to her feet by spraying water inside her nose. Another worker rolls a downed cow, bellowing and crying, in front of a farm vehicle and then drives over her head.[17]

The Humane Society exposing extensive abuse and the slaughter of numerous animals unable to walk at the Westland/Hallmark Meat Company in Chino, California, led to the plant closing and "the largest meat recall on record—143 million pounds."[18]

For most cows, though, death is more routinized. As discussed in chapter 4, much like the making of other products in our post-industrialized world, we have broken down the process of killing cows—the making of meat—into multiple tiny steps done over and over and over by workers, knives, and machines. Each human is responsible for only one small part of meat's production. This allows for the killing of thousands of animals per day at a given meat factory or slaughterhouse. Indeed, in the United States each day, 7,000 calves, 130,000 cattle, 360,000 pigs, and 24 million chickens are slaughtered.[19] That is a lot of killing.

Federal law mandates that the killing of cows happen at slaughterhouses in the following manner. First the cow is herded and probed through a chute into a "knocking box," a small space where they are held tightly and stunned, or they are herded one by one on a conveyor belt into a restrainer. The conveyor belt carries the animal to the person whose job it is to stun cows, the aptly titled "stun operator" or "knocker." This person has a compressed-air gun with which he or she shoots the animal in the forehead. The gun drives a steel bolt into the cow's skull and then retracts it. If the gun is sufficiently powered, well maintained, and properly used by the operator, it knocks the cow unconscious or kills the animal on the spot. The "shackler" chains the animal. This person's entire job is to put a chain around one of the cow's hind legs—hundreds of cows each day. The chain is attached to a powerful machine that lifts the cow by its leg into the air, and carries the cow, upside-down, through the next stages of the slaughtering process.[20]

Next, a person called the "sticker" cuts the cow's throat, specifically, the carotid arteries and jugular vein. Eisnitz explains,

> The sticker makes a vertical, not horizontal, incision in the animal's throat, near where the major vessels issue from the heart, to cut off the flow of blood to the animal's brain.
>
> Next the cow travels along the "bleed rail" and is given several minutes to bleed out. The carcass then proceeds to the head-skinners, the leggers, and on down the line where it is completely skinned, eviscerated, and split in half.[21]

The federal government passed the first version of this killing process into law with the Humane Slaughter Act in 1958, and updated it in 1978 and 2002.[22] The Humane Slaughter Act demands that animals be made unconscious in one blow—or rather stun—of a device. Only after being made quickly unconscious can the animals be shackled and hung up to be processed into meat.[23]

All laws aside, what *actually* happens to both cows—and humans—at the kill is another story.

The Jungle

In 1906, Upton Sinclair published his famous novel about an immigrant family new to Chicago and carrying the American dream. As we witness this family struggle to survive, the dream unravels, and the American reality for new immigrants and the working poor is revealed.[24]

The Jungle came out of Sinclair's profound political commitments. Sinclair was a lifelong radical and activist, and he expressed his politics through his writing. Theodore Roosevelt called Sinclair, and many other progressive journalistic writers of his time, a "muckraker." It was not a compliment. Roosevelt was referring to, as scholar Maura Spiegel notes, "the character in John Bunyan's *The Pilgrim's Progress* ... who could 'look no way but downward, with a muckrake in his hands.'"[25] Beyond prolific, Sinclair wrote and published over 90 books and pamphlets, as well as innumerable articles. Through *The Jungle*, his most famous work, Sinclair revealed the underbelly of American capitalism.

Sinclair told a story in which healthy, strong human beings are battered by and wither away at their work. If they go into the slaughterhouses strong, they come out weak, maimed, or even dead. Sinclair described the youthful Jurgis, when he first arrives from Lithuania, as powerful and healthy and deeply naive. Through this character Sinclair intended to expose the terrible treatment of workers in the meat industry, particularly after the meatpacker's strike of 1904 that failed to change their working conditions. The meat industry broke Jurgis physically and emotionally. In the course of the novel, both Jurgis's body and his family came undone, not unlike the nonhuman animals that also poured into the slaughterhouse. His elderly father developed numerous open wounds and a terrible cough working in a "pickle room," and quickly died. Jurgis's young brother-in-law was eaten alive by rats one night in the packinghouses. Jurgis himself was badly injured by a runaway animal and never managed to fully regain his former health and strength.

Sinclair described the deceptive and unsafe practices of the Chicago meat industry and their complete lack of concern for the public's health. Every part of every animal was used to make some product to sell to the unsuspecting consumer. Even sick animals were used.

> It seemed that they must have agencies all over the country to hunt out old and crippled and diseased cattle to be canned. There were cattle which had been fed on 'whiskey-malt,' the refuse of the breweries, and had become what the men called "steerly"—which means covered with boils. It was a nasty job killing these, for when you plunged your knife into them they would burst and splash foul-smelling stuff into your face; and when a man's sleeves were smeared with blood, and his hands steeped in it, how was he ever to wipe his face, or to clear his eyes so that he could see?[26]

Upon discovering the real origins of their dinner, the American public was outraged. *The Jungle* revealed slaughterhouse conditions so shocking and meat so filthy that meat sales plummeted more than 50 percent, and President Theodore Roosevelt personally crusaded for enactment of the Federal Meat Inspection Act of 1906. That law and subsequent legislation established standards for plant sanitation and required federal inspection of all meat shipped interstate or out of the country.

Sinclair made vivid more than the health hazards birthed by the industry. Yet, although the public responded loudly to the filth in their meat, they did not respond to the abuse of workers who produced their meat, or the violence against the animals that became their meat. In contrast to the rapid enactment of the Federal Meat Inspection Act and the Federal Food and Drug Act, both passed the same year that the book came out, no legal or other formal changes were made on behalf of meat industry workers or of the animals-to-be-meat. As Sinclair himself said, "I aimed at the public's heart, and by accident I hit it in the stomach."[27]

Sinclair brought public attention to the quality of the meat we eat. And while this attention resulted in laws mandating cleaner meat in 1906, there is still work to be done today. As the Humane Society has pointed out, if downed and sick animals are being slaughtered and processed for meat, consumers are almost certainly eating the diseased meat from these sick animals. Children in US public schools seem to be the consumers of some of this possibly dangerous meat. The Hallmark Slaughterhouse, the plant that closed after the Humane Society exposed their abuse and slaughter of downed cows, provided a "significant amount of meat to the National School Lunch Program."[28] Thus the Humane Society believes that the National School Lunch Program has received and served a considerable amount of meat from downed and potentially sick cattle.

The Humane Slaughter Act

From the perspective of the meat industry, the Humane Slaughter Act is problematic because it creates rules that result in a loss of profit. It takes too much time to follow the Humane Slaughter Act's mandated procedure for killing animals. It takes time to properly stun an animal. It takes time to correct an improper stun. And of course it takes time to keep the line slow enough to protect the workers. However, too often, what actually occurs in an attempt to speed up production and increase profit is that animals do not get stunned properly, if they get stunned at all.

As discussed by Thompson in his essay on time, industrialization in wealthy nations within the Modern World System coincided with the development of a new time sense. Increasingly, time became "currency: it is not passed but spent."[29] Further, Benjamin Franklin clarified, "Since our Time is reduced to a Standard, and the Bullion of the Day minted out into Hours, the Industrious know how to employ every Piece of Time to a real Advantage in their different Professions: And he that is prodigal of his Hours, is, in effect, a Squanderer of Money ... *Time is Money*."[30] This way of experiencing time as money, clock time, gripped most aspects of modern life. In slaughterhouses today, the concern over the potential wasting of time—and with the loss of time, profit—helps explain the matter-of-fact everyday cruelty to animals and the profoundly unsafe working conditions for humans.

Along with the issue of time, there is a second concern over the potential loss of profit through stunning animals. Many in the meat industry believe that stunning an animal to the point of stopping its heart will make the meat less valuable. Blood retained in meat offers bacteria a good place to develop and thrive. And of course, harboring thriving bacteria means a shorter time span from kill to plate for meat, and this could mean that more meat goes bad before the industry is able to sell it. Yet it is an industry myth (and incorrect) that an animal's heart has to keep beating in order to pump all the blood from its muscles.[31] Eisnitz interviewed Bucky White, a meatpacker at the John Morrell plant in Sioux Falls, South Dakota, about this myth and the worry over "too dead" cattle. Bucky White said, "'We got a superintendent who claims the big bolt kills the cattle 'too dead' and they don't bleed properly ... I've headed [skinned the heads of] and stuck cattle for twenty-one years, and I've never heard of cattle being too dead.'"[32]

Fully stunning animals is good for the animal about to be slaughtered and also good for the workers processing its meat. The animal is processed with minimal suffering, and workers stay safer, as they stick, skin, and cut large animals that are dead and do not fight the meatpackers as they work.

In the early 1980s, numerous studies demonstrated that the amount of blood retained in meat has no relationship to whether one stops an animal's heart (kills it) or just stuns it. Nonetheless, because of the worry over "too dead" cows, management often kept the stun gun current turned down. White explained to Eisnitz that the knocking guns they used had two sizes of bolts, and plant management required that the smaller, less effective bolt be used.[33]

Eisnitz asked White how often alive and conscious cattle come through the stunning process. "The way I look at it," White said, "out of the 1,228 beef I stuck today, it would have been okay if a few were still alive. But it's all day. Constantly, all day, I get live cattle." When Eisnitz asked how he can tell that the cattle are alive and conscious, White said, "The live ones you could tell 'cause they're bellowing, blinking, looking around." In the month immediately before he spoke with Eisnitz, White was kicked in the mouth, nearly driving his tooth through his lip. He was also kicked behind his ear, above his eye, and under both arms on separate occasions.[34]

Eisnitz also met with USDA meat inspector, Kevin Walker, about his experience at Kaplan Industries, a slaughterhouse in Bartow, Florida. Before their meeting Walker had contacted Eisnitz by mail with his concerns. He claimed that cattle were being skinned alive at Kaplan Industries.

> "This is not only extremely cruel," he wrote, "but also very dangerous for the plant personnel who have to skin these kicking animals." Plant management knew about the problem, he said, but didn't want to correct it because that would mean slowing down the production line. "I have contacted a number of federal agencies but have been told there is nothing they can do. They also told me that the problems I described exist all over the country, that they are just a little worse at Kaplan's."[35]

Eisnitz was initially skeptical about Walker's claims. It was hard to believe that anyone would skin conscious cows, making a hard job harder, particularly while being watched by USDA meat inspectors. Eisnitz assumed Walker had seen involuntary reflexes; to the inexperienced, that might look like the kicking of a conscious animal. Eisnitz decided to look into the matter.[36]

Clearly, skinning alive and conscious animals violates the Humane Slaughter Act. Oddly enough however, the very group who is supposed to enforce the Humane Slaughter Act, the USDA, resists the Act and allies itself with the meat industry. Further, there are no penalties—no fines or possible prison time—for violating the Humane Slaughter Act. USDA meat inspectors are merely supposed to shut down the kill line until the slaughterhouse remedies the violations. Shutting down the kill line, even momentarily, cuts into company profits and that potential loss of profit is meant to keep the meat industry obeying the law.[37]

Unfortunately Eisnitz found that rather than forcing a shutdown, the USDA simply ignored nearly all violations of the Humane Slaughter Act. Eisnitz interviewed numerous workers at various levels of work inside American meat packing businesses and found that slaughterhouses are consistently violating the Humane Slaughter Act. Again and again different people involved in meatpacking with different companies reiterated similar stories. Cows were being skinned alive and conscious. Awake and aware pigs were regularly immersed in scalding water and boiled alive. One man who worked at John Morrell and Company stated:

> I've seen live animals shackled, hoisted, stuck, and skinned. Too many to count. Too many to remember ... It's just a process that's

> continuously there. I've seen shackled beef looking around before they've been stuck... I've seen hog in the scalding tub trying to swim... In the wintertime there are always hogs stuck to the sides of the floors of the trucks. They go in there with wires or knives and just cut or pry the hogs loose. The skin pulls right off. These hogs were alive when we did this. Animal abuse at Morrell is so commonplace nobody even thinks about it.[38]

And because the Humane Slaughter Act does not protect poultry in the United States, the USDA does not have to bother ignoring the brutal poultry-slaughtering process. Conscious chicken are normally bled out and scalded in boiling water (to loosen their feathers), and it is completely legal.[39]

Eisnitz interviewed David Carney to learn more about why the Humane Slaughter Act seems to be ignored in most slaughterhouses. Carney worked as a meat inspector for the USDA in an Ohio meatpacking plant and as the chair of the federal meat inspector's union, the National Joint Council of Food Inspection Locals. Carney stated, "There's a specific problem with enforcing the Humane Slaughter Act. That's because these large slaughtering operations are primarily concerned with productivity and profit ... They don't care about the effects on the animals. It's as if they're not even killing animals. They're 'disassembling' them, processing raw materials in a manufacturing operation."[40]

Carney explained that although the USDA meat inspectors have the authority to stop the slaughter process—the line—at a slaughterhouse if they witness a violation of the Humane Slaughter Act, they are rarely in the slaughter area of a plant. About this, Eisnitz asked Carney, "How often does someone go down to the slaughter area and look?" Carney responded, "And leave his station?" He continued, "If an inspector did that, he'd be subject to disciplinary action for abandoning his inspection duties. Unless he stopped the line first, which would get him into even more trouble. Inspectors are tied to the line." Eisnitz asked Carney what the procedure was for checking compliance with the Humane Slaughter Act. Carney simply stated, "There isn't one." Eisnitz said,

> "Hold on. You're telling me that inspectors have the authority to stop the line when they see humane violations, but basically, they're never allowed to see them?"
>
> "That's right," [Carney] said. "Inspectors are required to enforce humane regulations on paper only. Very seldom do they ever go into that area and actually enforce humane handling and slaughter. They can't. They're not allowed to."

> "Besides," he continued, "our inspectors are already overwhelmed with their meat inspection duties and the agency has never addressed the responsibility of humane slaughter."[41]

Eisnitz found that one slaughterhouse, Kaplan, was killing around six hundred cows every day: "Not as many as some of the nation's newer high-speed mega-operations, but still high enough to make it the largest beef slaughterhouse in Florida."[42] Yet according to Walker, the facility was in poor repair and simply could not even handle the slower line times, when they slaughtered only 50 to 70 cows an hour. This meant that when the line speed increased—typically when the foreman wanted to slaughter and process as many cattle as possible at the end of the day—the workers were unable to maintain the fast pace.[43]

Rushing at their work, stun operators would sometimes miss and knock the animal at the side of its head instead of straight on. Some of the improperly stunned cows responded by breaking free and running wildly through the plant. Most regained consciousness once they had been hoisted onto the rail. These animals, hanging by one leg, fought, twisted, and turned, trying to get free.[44]

Conscious animal or not, the overhead moving rail continued, and with it the cow moved to the next stage in the process—to the sticker. When the cow was conscious and fighting, and particularly when the line was moving fast, the sticker might not manage to cut the cow's throat in such a way that it bled out fast. Nonetheless, within seconds after being cut, the cow arrived at the head-skinners. Walker explained to Eisnitz that the skinner would sometimes realize "an animal is still conscious when he slices the side of its head and it starts kicking wildly. If that happens, or if a cow is already kicking when it arrives at their station, the skinners shove a knife into the back of its head to cut the spinal cord."[45]

Cutting the spinal cord paralyzes the animal from the cut cord down. However, the cow remained conscious and able to feel everything from the cut up. In other words, the paralyzed cow could no longer kick or fight—making the human worker significantly safer—but it could still fully feel the pain of having its head skinned.

Live cattle struggling and fighting as they were being processed into meat presented an extremely dangerous situation for the meat packers processing them. The workers were crowded together and unprotected, many carrying knives. It was a perfect set-up for accidents. Walker explained that sometimes animals would break free of their shackles and come crashing down headfirst to the floor 15 feet below, where other men worked. "It's a miracle that nobody's been killed. There were three in one day, one right after another. One hit a worker, just a glancing blow, broke his leg. I almost got crushed by a falling bull."[46]

Even beyond the physical health risks faced by slaughterhouse workers, research indicates that slaughterhouse work negatively impacts the workers' psychological well being. One sign of this comes in the form of increased crime in communities where slaughterhouses are located. In their research, Amy J. Fitzgerald, Linda Kalof, and Thomas Dietz refer to this as the "Sinclair hypothesis."[47] Early in the history of industrial slaughter, Sinclair himself made the connection between the work of slaughtering animals and increases in violent crime in the larger community. Sinclair writes, "Men who have to crack the heads of animals all day seem to get into the habit, and to practice on their friends, and even on their families, between times."[48]

Fitzgerald, et al. note that ethnographic studies of communities that contain large slaughterhouses provide evidence of "dramatic increases in crime that have outpaced increases in the population," including in the category of violent crime. In terms of violence, they write, "Most of the increases in violent crime rates have been attributed to increases in domestic violence and child abuse."[49] They suggest that the increase in family violence indicates "a connection between the victimization of animals and the victimization of less powerful human groups, such as children and women."[50]

In their study, Fitzgerald, et al. test the Sinclair hypothesis. This theory, they explain, "suggests that the work of industrial animal slaughter ... has a different effect on local communities than other forms of industrial work." About their research on the Sinclair hypothesis, Fitzgerald, et al. write,

> We examine the relationship between slaughterhouse employment levels and crime rates, controlling for the variables commonly proposed in the literature as associated with crime in communities, and we compare the effects of the slaughterhouse industry with other manufacturing industries that are similar in labor force composition, injury and illness rates, but different in that the materials of production are inanimate objects, rather than animals.[51]

In their study, as suggested by the earlier ethnographic studies, Fitzgerald, et al. find that slaughterhouses do indeed have a unique statistically significant relationship to increased crime rates in the communities surrounding the slaughterhouses. Communities with slaughterhouses experience higher crime rates. In contrast, the other manufacturing industries that they study do not have a significant relationship to crime rates going *up*. In sharp contrast to slaughterhouse communities, the only significant relationship that some of the other industries had to crime rates was a *decrease* in the rates of crime. Fitzgerald, et al. clarify:

> Controlling for the extraneous variables, slaughterhouse employment has significant effects on arrests for rape and arrests for other sex offences. Of the comparison industries, only iron and steel forging demonstrates a significant effect on arrests for rape, but it is a negative one. Thus, controlling for the other variables, an increase in employment in iron and steel forging is associated with a *decrease* in arrests for rape.[52]

It seems that slaughterhouses alter human and nonhuman animals alike.

Rendering cow

An end result of all of this routinized violence against animals is of course food: meat to be sold, money to be made. As with the making of meat, in the selling of meat, the logic of profit makes its demands. As a result, humans are not the only ones eating cow. In fact, until August 1997, even the cows ate cows. It is, as Pollan writes, "industrial logic—protein is protein."[53]

Cows ate cow that came from the process of rendering. The rendering industry developed around 150 years ago. Much of the profit to be made in cow results from it. According to former rancher Howard F. Lyman, "When a cow is slaughtered, about half of it by weight is not eaten by humans: the intestines and their contents, the head, hooves, and horns, as well as bones and blood. These are dumped into giant grinders at rendering plants, as are the entire bodies of cows and other farm animals known to be diseased."[54]

However not only farm animals are rendered. Euthanized pets such as the six or seven million cats and dogs put down in animal shelters each year, and also roadkill, are all transformed into something else. The whole mix, made up of 40 billion pounds of dead animals each year, is ground up and steam-cooked. The lighter fatty material floats to the top of the mix and then is separated out to be used for making candles, waxes, cosmetics, soaps, and lubricants. The renderers dry and pulverize the heavier protein material into a powder. This protein concentrate is used as an additive in almost all pet food as well as livestock feed.[55]

In a book the National Rendering Association (NRA) published, *The Original Recyclers*, the NRA proudly proclaims its role in eliminating waste via "recycling." Discussing the early meat industry, author Frank Burnham writes in *The Original Recyclers*, "As the kill rate rose in the nation's slaughter houses from tens to hundreds, even thousands, of animals per week ... without the renderer the problem of disposing of these inedible byproducts of the beef industry would have become one of horrendous proportions."[56] Happily, the rendering industry took care of the waste by turning it into something to sell. As Shukin notes, rendering allows capitalist biopower to return "animal matter to another round in the marketplace."[57]

In her work on rendering and animal capital, Shukin develops the thinking of social theorist Antonio Negri. Negri argues that time and human labor have become one, and notes "the impossibility of distinguishing the totality of life (of the social relations of production and reproduction) from the totality of time from which this life is woven ... [T]he entire time of life has become the time of production."[58] Shukin argues, "A limit in Negri's thinking thus appears in the form of the closed loop within which production and human labor definitionally refer back to and reinforce one another ... There is little room in Negri's humanist philosophy of immanence to account for the material labors and lives of other species that have also become coextensive with the reproduction of capital."[59] For Shukin, nature—with human life and labor embedded in it—is subsumed "into the ontological conditions of capitalist production."[60]

Rendering offers a perfect example of capitalist biopower. Shukin illuminates, "More than just mopping up after capital has made a killing, the rendering industry promises the possibility of an infinite resubjection ('return') of nature to capital. The 'industrial ecology' metaphor of the closed loop valorizes the ecological soundness of waste recovery and recycling just as the rendering industry effectively opens up a renewable resource frontier for capitalism."[61] Animal life, indeed all life, is subsumed in capital.

Following "industrial logic," as Pollan writes, the meat industry fed "rendered cow parts back to cows," that is until "scientists realized that it was spreading mad cow disease." At that point the Food and Drug Administration banned feeding cows cow, or at least most of a cow cannot be fed to cows. "The FDA's rules against feeding ruminant protein to ruminants makes exceptions for 'blood products' (even though they contain protein) and fat." Further, the rules still allow "feedlots to feed nonruminant animal protein to cows. (Feather meal is an accepted cattle feed, as are pig and fish protein and chicken manure.)"[62]

Rendering brings beautiful clarity to the basic scientific idea that my 11-year-old recently learned in his physics class: matter does not disappear, it always, only, changes into something else. Given this physical reality, public health promoters worry that "since the bovine meat and bone meal that cows used to eat is still being fed to chickens, pigs, and fish, infectious prions (proteins implicated in the transfer of mad cow disease) could find their way back into cattle when they eat the protein of the animals that have been eating them."[63] Truly, we are what we eat.

I remember cows from all angles: individual cows, big, gentle beasts; dusty, dirty, mooing masses of cow; and chopped, red cow parts filling a gruesome freezer in my grandfather's garage.

In the twentieth century, men dominated the work of raising and killing farm animals, and women dominated the work of buying and cooking them (although often with a wage brought into the households by men). So the meat industry focused much of their advertising on women. And they did so with great success.

The women did the cooking in my family. Indeed for my grandmothers, their lives revolved around it. And they cooked meat at the heart of every meal. A meal really was not a meal without meat, particularly red meat. Only on Fridays did both my grandmothers abstain from meat and serve fish (for some reason fish did not count as meat until my generation came of age).

Although I am a vegetarian now, I used to love meat. I remember the perfect mix of chewy and soft flesh in my mouth, the wet of blood spilling out on my plate, and the flavor that blood added to bread and baked potato. I knew food mattered. As a Catholic, I was very familiar with the importance of eating the body and drinking the blood of Life. I knew that life reproduced itself in food and through eating. God himself—and in my childhood God, along with anyone else who had any power, was a man—God himself ate and was eaten.

Many of the problems in the beef industry stem less from the meat itself as from the system within which the meat is produced. Ranchers frantically raise cows, as many and as much cow as they can, to make some sort of a living in a system that gives its greatest rewards to those who control the killing and the dying, not the birthing and the living, of cow. The actual killers slaughter fast, fast, fast. Yet they too are mere cogs in the factory wheel producing meat and more meat. They, like the ranchers, make too little money, often far below a living wage. They risk their lives every day on the job, and not for something romantic like cowboys on the range. They risk serious injury by performing the same motion over and over all day long as they do their tiny part in transforming cow into meat.

The cows perhaps suffer most and for the least personal gain. Arguably, beef cows exist thanks to the beef industry. But a closer look at their lives makes it hard to argue that the modern beef cow's life is worth living. Looking at the immense suffering often involved in their deaths closes the case.

He gutted my sister's cat. And we watched, late at night, in our nightgowns, in the garage. And then he had us clean up the mess. The mess that was my sister's, my little sister's cat. I remember watching bloody guts go, swirling, down the toilet.

Chapter 8

And Violence

These are stories about how girls become girls. These are stories about seeing and not seeing, and about the role of violence in our lives. These are stories about my childhood.

As a child, I worked hard to be what I thought I should be as a girl: respectful and quiet, unquestioning, an accepter of rules rather than a maker of rules, "good." Yet beyond normative gender, I also worked to link the "reality," as I experienced it, with what I thought that reality meant. If I was sick, I worked to link the idea of being sick to the physical reality of being sick. I spent my childhood trying to bridge a gap between what was and what I understood, to bridge an enormous breach between a kind of truth, and the story we all lived in. All my efforts were like trying to reach one's hand across the Grand Canyon. I lived with an unbridgeable chasm between the violence that was happening, and the stories we simultaneously believed while the violence happened. And oddly, as life does, all the while life went on.

After my father killed my sister's cat, my sister, my brother, and I went on a planned vacation with our mother. Actually, my mother had already left for our vacation. She went ahead, while we three children and our animals—my sister's cat, Blackie; my cat, Thomasina; and our dog, Bear—stayed with my father in Grand Junction for a few days. Then my father flew my siblings and me in his little single engine airplane to meet my mother in California. (Incidentally, that was the one and only time I have seen the Grand Canyon, when my father flew us over it on our way to California. The gap that canyon opens is wide, too wide for stretching an arm, a child's arm, any human arm, across.) The plan was that he would care for our animals while we were away.

When we returned to Grand Junction, Wyoming, in my mother's little blue Volvo, we found, we decided, we believed that my sister's cat Blackie had run away. That was the story that we lived with for nearly 15 years; my sister's cat had run away. Of course, we never saw that cat again. And we lived with that story—we held it to be true—until my sister and I were both adults and another, the other, story appeared again. More violent than merely appearing, that other story burst through and irreparably ruptured the thin façade we maintained, the façade covering what really was with the story we told ourselves.

My Not-Eating Sickness

When I was ten, I became sick with some kind of flu. Or, maybe, I was not sick. I could not be sure. What was, and what was not real, evaded me. For example, I never quite knew if I actually did have a headache. Maybe I was just making it up. Even pain was disputable. Ultimately, there was only one thing I did know, simply know. I knew there was something deeply wrong with me. Or really, what was wrong went deeper than being wrong with me. The truth, the only truth, was that I, my self, was wrong. I was simply wrong.

So I cannot say, positively, that I was really sick that time when I was ten. But when I was a child I believed if someone were sick, if I were sick, I would have certain specific symptoms. These symptoms would be proof of my sickness. One of these symptoms was not eating. Among other things, I believed sick people did not eat.

So when I was ten and sick, I stopped eating. I stopped eating to be sure that I was really sick. I did not tell my mother about this decision. I did not tell anyone. Although really, apart from my mother, I had no one else to tell. I just stopped eating. I would not even eat my favorite things. Not even corn. Not even candy. Not even soda pop. I remember my mother spoon feeding 7-Up, 7-Up I did not want, into my mouth. My mother was scared about my not eating.

During that time, that time of not eating, at first I read. I read curled up under lots of blankets. This was something I loved to do, and something I believed sick people did. So at first I read, and then, after a while, all I did was sleep. Maybe I was starving. Not only did I stop eating, but I also stopped wanting to eat. I still remember being in my body then. It, I, was limp, and very, very thin, almost gone. My body almost went away, and took me with it.

I remember my mother loading me into her car, her old blue Volvo station wagon. Eventually that car was destroyed in an accident. But we still had it then. Many things happened in that car, including my mother taking me to the doctor, that time that I was sick and stopped eating. Like me, the doctor could not be sure what was wrong. But, he said, if she doesn't start eating, we will have to feed her intravenously. This I remember. Then, my mother and I went home.

My mother left my father when I was six. She left my father and went back to school, so she could build a life for herself, so she could support us. I already told you that my mother was brave. And I loved her immensely. I still do.

At this time, this time of my not-eating sickness, we lived in a small house on Ord Street. It was a rented house, and we lived there with my mother's lover Joe. Joe paid the rent. We had no money. My mother had left my father four years earlier. She kept Martin, Annie, and me. He kept the money. Unlike us, my father had a lot of money. But we were poor. So we lived in a small house with Joe and his two sons, Chris who was crazy mean and Joey who was my age. It was a bad time.

It was a bad time and bad things happened in that time. Like Chris. Joe's son Chris was simply a bad thing. Chris was crazy mean. Chris was like Clarke. Chris was cruel. Years later, when we were all grown and that time long over, we heard Chris had been arrested for jumping out at women from behind bushes. And then, we heard he had become a psychologist.

Chris was simply a bad thing. He was mean. He was mean to my mother. He was mean to me and my sister and brother. He was very mean. And one day, one afternoon when no one was home, Chris forced me to do a terrible, bad thing. He held me down and forced his penis in my mouth. Chris was cruel. And I was afraid, very afraid of Chris. I never told. I was too afraid. Like I said, it was a very bad time.

To Speak of My Mother

When I was six, my mother decided to divorce my father. I did not experience this as a change that needed explaining. I was a child. And to me, everything that was, simply was. Each moment, each happening, accounted for itself without explanation. As I said, I worked to link what was, the "reality" as I experienced it, with what I thought that reality meant. I did not question what was. Maybe this is because, having only known six years, I had little with which to compare my experience. I had my family and the places of six years. I did not know there had been other happenings, other years, other families. My world, its time and place, unfolded arrogantly sure that it was all there was.

So when I was six, my mother got a divorce. She got a divorce from my father. And this upset my grandmother. Upset is too mild a word. Yet any other word would not be polite enough for my grandmother. And really, I am not sure what the divorce meant to my grandmother. Did the divorce mean pain? Was the divorce a sign of her, my being-divorced-father's mother, failure in raising her son? Or was the divorce simply not okay because it was a doing of what my grandmother could not do? My mother divorced my father. She did what my grandmother could not, would not ever do. Was my grandmother angry?

When I was six, my mother divorced my father. It was a bad thing, something women should never do. It meant my mother was a Bad Woman. In our small town of Grand Junction, the knowledge of badness spread quickly. It spread as quickly, as thoroughly as water when you knock over a glass. Not wine, but water. For there was no dark stain to point to, no funny smell, no sign. Being bad cannot be seen, not in that way. I should know. Nor is being bad a profession, like being a teacher or doctor. It has no title. It just is. It is bigger, deeper, fainter than titles. It is simply known. And that is worse. My mother divorced my father when I was six. And then, it was known, she became someone else.

When my mother divorced my father, when I was six, my grandmother stopped talking to her. But it was more than that. My grandmother would not talk to my mother, she would not talk about my mother, she would not hear talk of my mother. Even my mother's picture, taken in her white wedding gown when she was still beautiful and Good and spoken of, came off the wall where it hung by the stairs, the stairs one took to go to The Girls' Room, the basement, or the rose garden. The picture came off the wall and left a clean spot behind, marking its place. The picture, like my mother, did leave a mark in its disappearance.

Did they tell me, someone, sometime, that I was not to speak of my mother? Ever. To my grandmother. Because this I knew. This was one of those not many things I knew. I knew it was Bad to speak of my mother in the presence of my grandmother. If I did so, I was to be ashamed. Even more ashamed than I already was.

Other people knew about my mother's Badness. Not only my grandmother knew. For as I said, such knowledge spreads. Quickly. Like spilled water, almost as soon as the spill happens, it is everywhere. I remember my friend Lindsey's mother indicating to me, somehow, without actually saying it, that she knew. Lindsey's mother was a Good Christian. This made her an authority on the issue of Badness. Of course, by then, by the time I was friends with Lindsey, when I was in the fourth grade and finally for a period of time beginning to have friends, by this time my mother had done another bad thing. By this time, my mother had moved in with Joe. And they weren't married. This, it was known, was Dirty, a sin. And Lindsey's mother told me so without telling me in words. My mother was Dirty. Somehow my mother's dirtiness made Lindsey's mother's not-dirtiness all the more profound. In fact, probably without someone like my mother around to be Dirty, Lindsey's mother might never have had the triumph of being, herself, Clean. At any rate, I was in the fourth grade and Lindsey's mother made all this clear to me, without actually saying it.

Her name was Mrs. Gray. And she was not only Clean, she was also scary. I knew, because she made sure I knew in her way without saying so, that I was lucky she let me play with Lindsey. It was risky. She was taking a risk that some of my mother's Badness, through me, might rub off on Lindsey. Lindsey's mother knew because it is known that Badness runs in families. If my mother was Bad, then I was too. I guess it's like they say, the apple never falls far from the tree. At any rate, the risk was that Lindsey might catch Badness, like catching a flu, from me. So Mrs. Gray was not only Clean, she was Kind. You would not have known it if she did not tell you, without saying it in words, you would not have guessed that Mrs. Gray was Kind. But she was, she made sure I knew. And due to her Kindness, she let Lindsey play with me. I was both grateful and scared. I was grateful because I knew, I knew before Mrs. Gray ever told-me-without-saying-it, I knew that I was Wrong. It, my wrongness, was something inexplicable but true, complete, absolute, and final. I myself, inside, was wrong. This I knew. So, naturally, I was grateful that Mrs. Gray let Lindsey play with me.

And I was scared. I was scared of Doing Something Wrong. I was scared my wrongness would spill, out of control, into my time with Lindsey. I was scared of Mrs. Gray. Once Mrs. Gray told Lindsey that if she were not home on time, on time meant whenever Mrs. Gray told Lindsey to be home, that she, Mrs. Gray, would come after Lindsey. Mrs. Gray said she would come after Lindsey with a belt. Then Lindsey would regret her lateness. I imagined Mrs. Gray, bent over slightly, carrying a big leather belt, her face, as it always was, cramped in angry bitterness, searching the streets of Grand Junction for Lindsey. I imagined her beating Lindsey nearly to death. Of course, she would not beat Lindsey until she died, just until she nearly died. For if Lindsey died, then Mrs. Gray would not have the satisfaction of Lindsey's regret. Once dead, no one regrets anything. Dead is dead. But nearly dead is a good place for regret. I did not like Mrs. Gray.

The Closet

When I was a child, before I met Lindsey, I did not have friends. My mother and I share a memory about this. My mother remembers driving by my elementary school in Grand Junction, Beitel Elementary School, one day when the children were outside, playing, during recess. She remembers driving by and seeing the children playing outside, and then seeing me. I was not playing. I was not with the other children. I was sitting, alone, on a bench near the school wall, just sitting. I was sitting alone watching the other children play. She remembers how it made her hurt inside to see me there, to see me there alone.

I remember too. I remember watching the children play. I remember sitting on a bench, alone during recess, watching the other children play. I remember. I remember waiting, alone on the bench, for time to pass so that I could go home. I remember alone.

When I was a child, I had an alone place that was just mine. It was in the room I shared with my sister, when we shared a room at our house on Rainbow Street. It was in the first of two rooms we shared on Rainbow Street. This room was upstairs right next to my parents' room before they got a divorce, before my dad made us move out of that house so that he could live there with his new wife. This room had two beds and two closets and two little girls, my sister and me.

My sister was messy and I was neat. This has not changed. She is still messy. I am still neat. Being neat, I did not want her mess on my side of the room. Being messy, she didn't care whether either my neatness or her messiness crossed any room boundaries. As the one who cared, I enforced the room boundary. I enforced the room boundary, one side was hers and one side was mine. And I wished desperately for my own room.

I want to tell you that in that room on Rainbow Street, that room that I shared with my sister, that room with a boundary marking her side from mine, I did make a private place for myself. I made a private place in the closet. I made the closet into a room of my own. And I would sit in there, quietly, for hours.

My sister and I each had our own closet. The closets were along one wall, across from our twin beds. When one entered the room, first on one's right was Annie's closet and on the left, Annie's bed. Then after crossing over the boundary separating her half of the room from mine, one came to my closet on the right and my bed on the left. And finally, there was a window on the wall across from the door, next to my bed. That window looked out on the front lawn and on Rainbow Street.

So, in the room that I shared with my sister, I had a closet of my own. The closet had a door that opened and shut, just like any regular door, as though the closet were a regular room. And when one opened the door there was a light in the closet that went on automatically. You did not have to ask that light to turn on. It knew to go on, right away, when the door was opened. That light knew that nobody likes to be in a dark closet. I could open the door and go into the closet and sit, with the door not all the way shut, so that the light stayed on. I could sit in that closet, all alone. And I did. I would sit in that closet, all alone, for hours. It was mine.

I put a small chair in the closet, a small chair that my grandmother had given me. It was wooden and had my name, Jeannie, painted in dark blue across the part where you rest your back. I put pictures on the walls. I put my favorite books in the closet. I even kept my hamster in there. For a while, I let my hamster go wild in that closet. It seemed only fair to let my hamster have full use of the space. My cat had full use of the space outside of the closet. She could even go outside of the house. And she did. When she wanted back into the house, she would jump up and grab hold of the front door knob with one paw, with her other paw she would pound impatiently on the doorbell. Hearing the noisy ringing of the bell, someone would go to answer the door. Whoever it was would swing the door open with my cat, Thomasina, still clinging to the knob. The door opener was always fooled, for a moment, into thinking there was no one there. It was a ghost or a trick or something. And then, Thomasina would let go of the knob, gracefully landing on her feet to walk nonchalantly in through the open door.

So this was a fair compromise. It was a fair compromise that the hamster have a space of her own, a space where she could be, at least a little bit, free. Everyone needs some freedom. But the hamster began to abuse her privileges. She began to eat big chunks out of the bottom of the closet door. It wasn't that I minded. I was sure the hamster had her reasons. And the chunks did not stop anything from happening. The door was still a door. The hamster still a hamster. I really did not mind a few big chunks in my closet door. My father, however, would have minded were he to discover the chunks. And I was scared of my father. I was scared of his anger. My hamster did not know my father. She did not know to be afraid. Otherwise, maybe I could have convinced her to stop her project. But as it was, as I had no way to explain the situation to the hamster, I had to put her back in her cage.

The Shadow

I have no idea where it all came from. I have no idea why my family, our history going back, back and back in time, is so seeped in hurting. I don't know. I really don't know.

Many things happened that I do not understand. They happened behind the curtain separating real from unreal. They were hidden happenings. And yet they were. They were.

When I was six, my mother divorced my father. He did not want the divorce. She did. She wanted to have her life. She fought to have her life. My mother was brave. She still is.

Around this time, the time of the divorce, other things happened too. Before the divorce and after too, a shadow began coming to my room. This shadow would come in the night. During the night, when everyone was asleep and all was dark and cold and quiet, this shadow would come to my room. It would creep around the corner from the hall, through the door, to my bed. This shadow would come to my bed. And I was afraid. This shadow would do bad things. And I was afraid.

Clear in my memory is the door to my room. My bed faced that door. Opening my eyes, I could see the door without moving. I could watch and wait, afraid. Afraid. Clear in my memory is the corner, near the door, up and across from my bed. I came to know that corner well. Sharp lines emerging from a single point. If you have ever stared intensely at a corner, you will know what I mean. A lot can happen in such a small, simple place.

At this time we still lived in the Rainbow Street house. But now, my sister and I were in a different room. We were no longer in the room with the two closets and the window looking out on Rainbow Street. We shared a room in the basement. It was a big room in the basement at the end of a long hall. My brother had his room there too, next to ours, in the basement at the end of the long hall. And there was a bathroom. It was the bathroom where, later, my sister and I would clean up her cat. And there was a laundry room. Thomasina had her one litter of kittens in that laundry room. She had two kittens in the litter. And she was a terrible mother. She really wanted nothing to do with the kittens. Not everyone is meant to be a parent. So after those kittens, poor unwanted things, we had Thomasina fixed. She was not meant to be a parent. And there was a storage room down in that basement too. The storage room was scary, full of cement and pipes and long forgotten things. The storage room was scary.

I don't know where my sister was when the shadow came. Maybe she was there, in the bed next to mine, maybe she wasn't. She was so little, only three. And I was little too. I was six years old. I don't know where my sister was when the shadow came. But I do know that I would disappear. When the shadow came, I would disappear. I would go away. I would go away to nowhere. I would disappear. And the shadow did not care. I was both there, and not there, for the shadow. I did not matter. I was not the point. So I would go away when the shadow came. I would go away and leave my body behind. My body, small under the covers on my bed, was all. My body was all that shadow would find.

No one, only I, knew about the shadow. And I was afraid. I was afraid to tell. And so I never did. Until now.

But it's hard to know with memories. They are not photographs, to be held on to, to be shown, to be put away. It's hard to know with memories. Yet as far as I remember, as far as I remember that shadow came and, after a time or two, after a year or two, after a while, the shadow stopped. And life, as it does, went on.

Clarke

Clarke knew that the divorce was a Bad Thing. He tried to keep the divorce from happening. He tried to keep the divorce from emerging out into the world, out into a place where everyone would be forced to see that Something Was Wrong. When he heard, when he heard about my mother, about my mother wanting to live, he got in his car and drove to Grand Junction. As soon as Clarke heard, he got in his car and drove the two and a half hours from Kidron to Grand Junction. He came in the evening. And I don't think he even stayed the night. He was not there for a visit. He had come to give my father a message. And the message was not to let this happen. The message was not to allow the divorce. What my mother wanted was not the point.

Yet the divorce did happen. And really, even so, even with the divorce, it took a long time for us; it took a long time for us to really see. One has to learn to see.

My grandmother, my Gram Brennan, used to say, this too shall pass. And she was right.

My Gram grew old. She grew old in every way, in every way a person can be old. And now she is dead. Yet long before that final giving up, my grandmother gave up remembering, maybe even before I knew her. My grandmother gave up remembering a long time ago. And so even though I knew her, I really never did. You cannot know someone without memories. For, in so many ways, we are our memories. Our memories make us. From them, we become.

And my other grandmother, my father's mother, is dead. And somewhere, somewhere in the midst of it all, the time went. The time went away, and took my story with it.

My grandmother used to say, this too shall pass. This too shall pass. And she was right.

Chapter 9

There Is No Returning Home

My family did not merely make a small fortune off of meat. We ate it too. For all the problems that meat and the meat industry present, it is not only a problem. Meat is also food. As in the case of meat, violence does more than deaden. Because nothing disappears, violence like meat offers a challenge, a resistance to the order of things. And in the case of meat, the result of violence is a gift of sorts from the cows, and from the labor and the land. And those who do eat meat devour it and are, at least a little bit, renewed. And the cows die unto us, and eventually we to the land, and the land feeds. And we begin again.

When I went to visit my grandmother Clarke years ago, for the first and last time in a long time, Clarke was dead. He had died a few months before, in 1993. Where he went I cannot say. I don't know if he ever really left that house. But at any rate, he was definitely dead. And I was glad. His dying let me come, one last time, to see my grandmother. Even if it was too late.

I went to Kidron for one day that time, for one day only. By then I would no longer stay the night in my grandmother's house. So I just went for the day, on my way from other places to other places. Yet when I arrived, my grandmother did not know me. She did not know the me that I had become. The visit was too late.

I returned to Kidron with my stepmother, my father's wife, Lydia. Lydia picked me up at the bus stop in Spokane the morning of my visit. I had come into Spokane after an overnight bus ride from Bozeman, Montana, where my mother lived. I got off the bus bewildered, small. Somehow, although I was an adult by then, by that day I went to visit my grandmother, somehow I was still too small. I was still too small for the circumstances of my life. And my life, my life was much too big for me. But maybe that is how it always is with pain.

When I climbed out of the big smelly bus, there was Lydia waiting for me. She had come to pick me up in her fancy gray car. It was a Porsche, or a BMW, or something. It was one of those cars you are supposed to want to have. It had leather seats and that new car smell. I prepared myself to be sick all the way to Kidron.

My arrival in Spokane this time was not the same as it used to be. This arrival was not the arrival of my childhood, when I would go to visit my grandmother for two weeks in the summertime. Both I and the arrival had changed. Lydia, not my grandmother, met me to drive me back to Kidron. Lydia greeted me with a hug. She asked if I wanted to eat or use the restroom. It was a strange greeting, strange because it was not strange enough. It was not the greeting of a stepmother and stepdaughter who have not seen each other for four years. Nonetheless, after 12 hours on the bus, I did need to go to the bathroom. And I wanted to wash that bus smell off of me before seeing my grandmother. Afterwards, still smelling faintly of bus, Lydia took me to get a cup of coffee at a nearby fast food restaurant. The restaurant was busy and dirty and full of angry people. Some man was rude to Lydia. I ordered my coffee to go, and we quickly left.

I cannot say for certain, but I think Lydia was as uncomfortable as I. Climbing into her car, we knew we had one and one half hours ahead, just the two of us, alone. I felt stiff in my body, as though the me that was alive had gone. The me that spoke and chose things, that took up space, had disappeared. Or maybe, that me was tucked away somewhere, somewhere safe. Maybe I was tucked away somewhere in my body, maybe in my right shoulder, which is my perpetually stiff shoulder. It is the shoulder from which my headaches come. It makes sense to me that the place where pain comes from is where I would be. Anyhow, wherever I had gone, the rest of me was left behind to sit, scared, in Lydia's car for a one and one half hour long drive to Kidron.

I asked Lydia how she was. When she answered, I remember her as relieved. My question was a start. And the time began. And we drove. While we drove, Lydia talked. I think she talked the whole way. But the time, our drive to Kidron, in my memory is a blur. I just remember her talking, her voice as a background while I looked out the window watching Wyoming, the plains, go by.

I don't know if you have ever been somewhere both deeply familiar, and very far away. It is a peculiar kind of coming home. Looking out the window, I was startled at how well I knew this place. I was startled at my love for it. I had forgotten. I had forgotten because I had no other choice.

And Lydia talked. She told me about herself, about her life, about her friends, and her job and what she had been doing. She had started taking antidepressants and going to psychotherapy, so she told me about that too. She told me about her relationship with my father. At this time, the time of my final visit to my grandmother, Lydia and my father were split up. My father had left Lydia. He had left her although she did not want to be left. At any other point in the history of my family, at any time up until this time, my father leaving Lydia would have been an enormous event. Not because of my father and Lydia. Not because they loved each other so very much or even at all. My father leaving Lydia would have been an enormous event because marriages were supposed to be for always, like it or not. Getting married was a deal one made with God. The other person did not really matter. But God, one did not back out of deals with God.

Well, my father started to back out of his deal with God. He left Lydia, for a while. And then, he came back. But at this time, at the time of my final visit to my grandmother, my father had only left. He had yet to come back. At the time of my final visit to my grandmother, I was not sure that my father would ever come back to Lydia. One does not always come back. Sometimes one leaves forever.

So as we drove, Lydia talked about my father, about his leaving her, about her wishing he had not left, about her hoping he would come back. She talked and talked. I know I said that the drive, the drive to my grandmother's house, was a blur. However, blurry as it was, I know that Lydia talked about my father because, at this time, this time of him leaving her, she invariably talked about my father. In fact, not only did she perpetually talk about my father at this time, but she only talked at this time. Or actually, she only talked to me at this time. What I am trying to tell you is that Lydia and I had not spoken for almost four years. Then, my father left Lydia. And then, after almost four years, she called me.

My father left Lydia. And that is when Lydia called me. I was in Boston living in the living room, on the couch, of some friends. I was lost. One might think that Lydia called me because she too was lost, lost without my father. But it could not have been that, that Lydia called me because she knew about our mutual lostness. Lydia had not spoken with me for almost four years, so she did not know how I was. What I am trying to tell you is that I am not sure why Lydia called me. I don't know why she called me. And I especially don't know why she called me at this time, this time of my father leaving her. But she did.

I was very surprised to pick up the phone and hear her voice, her voice on the other end. I said, hello? And she said, Jean it's Lydia. Lydia? I said. Yes, she said. Your father left me, she said. Oh, I said. Oh. I'm sorry. And then we spoke. We spoke then for the first time in nearly four years. Four years are not always a long time, but these four years were. In these four years many things had happened, so they were a long four years. It had been a long time.

I cannot really tell you what else was said in that conversation with Lydia, that first conversation in four years. I was too surprised to hold the words in my head. But she called me. This I know. And after that, after that first call, she called me quite a lot. Lydia called me every couple of weeks after that first call. She was having a hard time. She missed my father. Or, at least, she wanted him back. I cannot say for certain that she missed him. But anyhow, she missed the idea of him, of him being there, with her. She felt alone. Or maybe, she simply realized how alone she had always felt. So she called me. She did not only call me. She called my sister, Annie, and my brother, Martin. She also called my half-brother, her son, Timothy. But there was nothing unusual about that. She had been calling him all along.

Out of these calls was born my visit to my grandmother. Well, not just the calls. There was another thing. At that time of my father leaving Lydia, something else happened. Clarke died. So, in a sense, at the same time that my father left Lydia, Clarke left my grandmother. And because Clarke had left, I could go back. And so I did, one last time.

Gram's House

So it was Lydia who drove me to my grandmother's house for my final visit. It was a very lonely day. When we arrived, my grandmother was waiting. My Aunt Clara and her daughter Stephanie were there too. Lydia had told them I was coming, so they also came for lunch. Maybe they came to make the whole thing less uncomfortable. Or to make me more comfortable. Stephanie was no longer a baby. Once, when she was two, she escaped and ran two blocks away stark naked. They found her, shopping, at a neighbor's garage sale. That was Stephanie. This person, just starting college, sullen and shy with her finger nails painted gray, I did not know. At first I wished they were not there. I wanted time alone with my grandmother. But in the end it did not matter.

In the end it didn't matter who was there. My grandmother did not recognize me anyhow. When we pulled up in front of the house, she was waiting in the door. Her back was bent. This made her much smaller. From then, her back only bent more, curving over, forcing her into herself. But at this time, already it was a problem. A few months before, when Clarke was on one of his many final stays at the hospital in Spokane, my grandmother had rented a room nearby. She wanted to be close to him. One day, alone in her room, in a town where she knew no one, she fell out of her bed. She fell, and could not get up. Her bent back would not uncurl itself so that she could pull herself onto her feet. And because she was alone in a room in a town where she knew no one and no one knew her, there was not a soul to help her. Like I said, she was alone. So she lay there, on the floor, for hours. We do not know how long she lay there. Luckily, my father and my brother happened to be visiting my grandfather in the hospital that day. They had driven over from Grand Junction. After seeing Clarke, they came by my grandmother's room and found her on the floor. She could not tell my father how long it had been, or even what had happened. She was confused, confused after so many hours lying on the floor, lying curled up, lying helpless.

When my brother told me the story—and it was he who told me because by then I had no contact with my father—when he told me the story, I understood about my grandmother's confusion. My brother attributed her confusion to being old. But I knew it was not that. I knew to say she was confused because she's old is the same thing as telling someone they are sad because they're tired. My grandmother was old when she fell on the floor and couldn't get up. But being old and being confused are not the same thing. Most of us, while not old, are confused. But anyhow, let me tell you the reason for my grandmother's confusion. My grandmother was confused because she had spent too many hours lying on the floor, too many hours helpless. Helplessness forces one into a kind of letting go that can be very confusing. I don't think it's confusing for everyone, but certainly for someone like my grandmother it would be. As far as I can tell, my grandmother spent her whole life holding on. So after a lifetime of gripping tightly, to fall down, to be forced into lying helpless on the floor, for hours, would be confusing.

After that my father and his brothers would no longer let her stay in that room, by herself in Spokane. They made her stay at home in Kidron. And they hired a caretaker to stay with her all the time. This was not what my grandmother wanted. But even though she was their mother, even though they were her children, she had no choice. They did not give her any choice. It was for the best, Lydia said.

When Lydia and I arrived at my grandmother's house for my last visit there, my grandmother was standing bent in the door. She was waiting for us. She used to do this when I was a child. Seeing my grandmother waiting in the door always made me feel welcome, always made me feel wanted. With my grandmother, I belonged.

But on this visit, this final visit, things were different. I did not belong. I did not belong at my grandmother's anymore. I knew this as soon as I walked into the house and accepted my grandmother's greeting kiss. She did not know me. I did not belong. I am not sure how to explain the hurt of this to you. It is the hurt of displacement, of being too big, or too different or too something, and so, no longer having a place somewhere, somewhere that, at least at one time, mattered deeply. I really don't know how to tell you of this hurt for I cannot even describe it to myself. What I can say is that one day, a year or two after my final visit to my grandmother, I saw a set of kitchen glasses just like those my grandmother once had. They were her everyday glasses. They were for simple lunches and glasses of 7-Up while we played cards and things like that. When I saw those kitchen glasses, the ones just like my grandmother's, I knew how deep this indescribable hurt was, this indescribable hurt about my grandmother. It is a vast hurt.

At my grandmother's house that day with Lydia, everything had changed. At first, I thought that many of my grandmother's things were missing. Somehow the house seemed emptier. And maybe things were missing, things that had belonged to my grandmother. But it might just be that the magic of that house was gone. The magic was gone. And it had left behind a lot of empty places. After we ate lunch, I looked around the house, by myself, quickly. I was trying to find something, something to bring me back again. But nothing did. Nothing did. It was too late.

It's odd to realize, to know, that the choice was mine to leave. I was the one who went away. I was the one who went away so that I could never come back. In some way it is hard for me to understand that one, that I, can choose things such as this. It doesn't make sense that one would knowingly, really choosing, make a choice that entailed so much hurt.

Lydia and Timothy

My father met Lydia when I was six or seven years old. My mother had left him that year. So he met Lydia. It is odd to realize that when he met her, she was in her twenties. She was a young woman, just beginning life, younger than I am now. Except that there are big differences between me now and Lydia then. One difference is that Lydia was alone with her small son, Timothy, who became my half-brother. Timothy is a year older than me and a year younger than my brother, Martin. When my father married Lydia, he adopted Timothy. Timothy constitutes a big difference between Lydia then and me now. Yet there is an even bigger difference. The even bigger difference is fear. Lydia was afraid, and I am too. But, afraid as I am, I still make my own choices. I own my life, not fear.

So Lydia married my father when I was eight or so. Her condition was that my father adopt her son, Timothy. So he did. One thing you can say for Lydia, she sure loved Timothy. She was not the kind of person who would simply cop out on her own child to get a better deal for herself. She and Timothy were a unit. He was a part of the deal.

I first remember spending time with Timothy over at Lydia's house. My father would bring me over there for the evening. And, while he spent time with Lydia, Timothy and I played. Timothy has always been one of those people everyone likes. Even in our cliquey

Grand Junction Junior High School, Timothy had friends in every group, the jocks, the popular kids, the smart nerdy kids, the musical druggy kids, the Mexican American kids, the white kids, everyone. Everyone always liked Timothy. So, Timothy and I hit it off right away. I liked him too.

We spent those first evenings having marble races in Lydia's bathtub. We would lean over the edge of the empty tub, holding marbles at the top of the curvy comfortable end, the end where one leans back while soaking. After a tension-filled countdown, simultaneously we would let the marbles go, and then watch them race down and across the length of the tub until they crashed into the other side. Naturally, you wanted your marble to get there first. That was winning. It was a wonderful game. I have always liked marbles. I don't even mean the marble games so much as the actual marble. They hold such intriguing colors in their small round bodies. And they are capable of making such wonderfully alarming crashing noises. But also, marbles, small and solid perfect balls of glass, are simply pleasing to hold in one's hand. So, it was in part because of my affinity for marbles that I liked the game so much.

Yet it was more than that. It was Timothy. In a way Timothy was like my grandmother. In their presence, you felt that whatever you were doing was a treat, something special. At least I felt that way about my grandmother. But everyone felt that way about Timothy. Well, everyone except maybe my father. I don't think my father and Timothy ever hit it off. And, as wanted as he was everywhere else, I think that Timothy always felt like an outsider in our family. I think Timothy believed he did not belong in the family. But the truth was that no one belonged.

We did eventually learn to see, my mother and her three children. We learned to see what had happened on the other side of the story we had called reality. I am not sure how it happened. I am not sure why it happened to us and not to my father or my grandmothers or the many others in my family who died ensnared. Why do some fight to get free and others remain, caught, the wire holding them, forever, tightly.

I do wonder if, at least for some, at least for me, trauma acts as a force that pushes one towards some kind of freedom. Why me, why my mother, I do not know. Yet I do know that the trauma would not let me rest. And, although I could only see inches ahead into a very dark night, I kept moving.

Somehow life pushes for itself. It demands. It demands freedom.

Once, driving home from college across a mountain pass, I was caught in a blinding snowstorm. The snow was so thick, I might as well been underground, buried, deep in snow. I knew the road I could not see, the road I hoped I still was on, had other drivers travelling over the mountain pass, caught in snow. If I simply stopped where I was, played it safe and stayed put, they could see me no more than I could see them and were likely to drive right into me. Stopping was not an option. Moving forward did not seem an option either as I could not see the difference between road and no road, but I kept moving slowly, inch by inch, forward and somehow found my way through to the other side of snow, the other side of storm.

I cannot say how I found my way little by little without driving off the road, but I did. And here I am having survived the storm, on the other side of something. And now, I have a good life. I no longer live out west, surrounded by plains and mountains. I live in a city, with people all around, all the time. I have two delicious children. I have a partner and many friends. I have a job I love. I have a good life. How did I get here? And why me, and not my father and not my grandmother Brennan and not crazy Susan and not Clarke? I do not know. Yet it seems that trauma does more than kill, more than whirling, spinning, gutting-cats, sex-with-little-girls destruction; it also, sometimes, pushes life forward.

As Nikolas Rose suggests for us all, I am in so many ways actively shaping my own life, no longer tightly held by wire. It is a life that matters to me, for what it is, right now, and not only for some always-future goal. And I do hope that this book will offer at least a tiny crack in the wall of power, an opening of sorts, to others living in violence.

As to the cows, so many responses are possible. Yet the simplest is to stop eating them. In stark contrast to my growing up, my own children have never tasted meat. We are vegetarian. When I started to remember, I swore off killing once and for all.

Notes

1 Introduction

1. Cathy Caruth, *Unclaimed Experience: Trauma, Narrative, and History* (Baltimore, MD: The Johns Hopkins University Press, 1997), 4.
2. I am very grateful to Isaiah Halley-Segal for this comic strip; Scott Adams, *It's Obvious You Won't Survive by Your Wits Alone* (Kansas City, MO: Andrews and McMeel, 1995), 125.
3. For more information on pastoral farming, please do see Michael Pollan, *The Omnivore's Dilemma: A Natural History of Four Meals* (New York: The Penguin Press, 2006).
4. Daniel Imhoff, ed., *The CAFO Reader: The Tragedy of Industrial Animal Factories* (Berkeley, CA: Watershed Media, 2010).
5. Imhoff, *The CAFO Reader*, xiii.
6. Imhoff, *The CAFO Reader*, xiv–xv.
7. Paige Tomaselli and Meredith Niles, "Changing the Law: The Road to Reform" in Daniel Imhoff, ed., *The CAFO Reader: The Tragedy of Industrial Animal Factories* (Berkeley, CA: Watershed Media, 2010), 318.
8. Mark Bittman, "Some Animals Are More Equal Than Others," *New York Times*, March 15, 2011, <http://opinionator.blogs.nytimes.com/2011/03/15/some-animals-are-more-equal-than-others/?emc=eta1>.
9. David Bacon, "The Kill-Floor Rebellion," *The American Prospect*, June 30, 2002, <http://prospect.org/cs/articles?article=the_killfloor_rebellion>.
10. Imhoff, *The CAFO Reader*, 70.
11. Eric Schlosser, "Hog Hell: Smithfield's Workers Face a Modern-Day Jungle," *The Nation*, September 11, 2006.
12. Karen Olsson, "The Shame of Meatpacking," *The Nation*, September 16, 2002, 11–16.
13. Imhoff, *The CAFO Reader*, 78–79.
14. Imhoff, *The CAFO Reader*, xvii.

15. Imhoff, *The CAFO Reader*; Gail A. Eisnitz, *Slaughterhouse: The Shocking Story of Greed, Neglect, and Inhumane Treatment Inside the U.S. Meat Industry* (Amherst, NY: Prometheus Books, 1997).
16. Imhoff, *The CAFO Reader*, 69–70.
17. Michel Foucault, *Society Must Be Defended: Lectures at the College de France, 1975–1976* (New York: Picador, 2003), 252–253.
18. I am so thankful to Rafael de la Dehesa for this wonderful term.
19. Nikolas Rose, *Powers of Freedom: Reframing Political Thought* (Cambridge: Cambridge University Press, 1999), 282.
20. Rose, *Powers of Freedom*, 283.
21. Gilles Deleuze quoted in Rose, *Powers of Freedom*, 283; from Gilles Deleuze, *Essays Critical and Clinical*, trans. D. W. Smith and M. A. Greco (Minneapolis: University of Minnesota Press, 1997), 133.
22. Michel Foucault, *The History of Sexuality, Volume 1: An Introduction*, trans. Robert Hurley (New York: Vintage Books, 1978), 144.
23. Patricia Ticineto Clough with Jean Halley, eds., *The Affective Turn: Theorizing the Social* (Durham, NC: Duke University Press, 2007).
24. Nicole Shukin, *Animal Capital: Rendering Life in Biopolitical Times* (Minneapolis: University of Minnesota Press, 2009).
25. Foucault, *The History of Sexuality*, 141–142.
26. Nikolas Rose, *The Politics of Life Itself: Biomedicine, Power, and Subjectivity in the Twenty-First Century* (Princeton, NJ: Princeton University Press, 2007), 52.
27. Rose, *The Politics of Life Itself*, 53.
28. Foucault, *Society Must Be Defended*, 250.
29. Giorgio Agamben, *The Open: Man and Animal* (Stanford, CA: Stanford University Press, 2004), 15.
30. Michel Foucault, *The Birth of Biopolitics: Lectures at the College de France, 1978–1979* (New York: Picador, 2008), 147.
31. Foucault, *The Birth of Biopolitics*, 228.
32. Foucault, *The Birth of Biopolitics*, 229.
33. I am very grateful to Jacob Segal for all of his help in the thinking and writing of this paragraph.
34. Shukin, *Animal Capital*, 11.
35. Shukin, *Animal Capital*, 7.
36. Shukin, *Animal Capital*, 5.
37. Shukin, *Animal Capital*, 11.
38. Shukin, *Animal Capital*, 5.
39. Shukin, *Animal Capital*, 4.
40. Jimmy M. Skaggs, *Prime Cut: Livestock Raising and Meatpacking in the United States, 1607–1983* (College Station, TX: Texas A and M University Press, 1986), 3.
41. Skaggs, *Prime Cut*, 3.
42. Michel Foucault, *Discipline and Punish: The Birth of the Prison* (New York: Vintage Books, 1979).

43. Foucault, *Discipline and Punish.*
44. Jacob Segal, "Freedom and Normalization: Poststructuralism and the Liberalism of Michael Oakeshott," *American Political Science Review*, 97, no. 3 (August 2003): 447.
45. Jean Halley, *Boundaries of Touch: Parenting and Adult-Child Intimacy* (Champaign: University of Illinois, 2007), 2.

2 Where the Cows Came From

1. Frederick Jackson Turner, *The Frontier in American History* (Tucson: The University of Arizona Press, 1920/1994).
2. Patricia Nelson Limerick, *The Legacy of Conquest: The Unbroken Past of the American West* (New York: W. W. Norton and Company, 1987).
3. Limerick, *The Legacy of Conquest*, 18.
4. Michael Pollan, *The Omnivore's Dilemma: A Natural History of Four Meals* (New York: The Penguin Press, 2006), 71.
5. Jimmy M. Skaggs, *Prime Cut: Livestock Raising and Meatpacking in the United States, 1607–1983* (College Station, TX: Texas A and M University Press, 1986).
6. Skaggs, *Prime Cut*, 11.
7. Skaggs, *Prime Cut*, 11.
8. Skaggs, *Prime Cut*, 12.
9. Public Broadcasting Service (PBS), "New Perspectives on the West: Frederick Jackson Turner, 1861–1932," 2001. December 3, 2010, http://www.pbs.org/weta/thewest/people/s_z/turner.htm.
10. Turner, *The Frontier*, 3
11. Limerick, *The Legacy of Conquest*, 18.
12. Limerick, *The Legacy of Conquest*, 18–19.
13. Richard Slotkin, *Gunfighter Nation: The Myth of the Frontier in Twentieth Century America* (New York: HarperCollins Publishers, Inc., 1992), 11.
14. PBS, "New Perspectives on the West."

3 Where the Irish, Where My Family, Came From

1. Noel Ignatiev, *How the Irish Became White* (New York: Routledge, 1995).
2. Immanuel Maurice Wallerstein, *The Modern World-System: Capitalist Agriculture and the Origins of the European World-Economy in the Sixteenth Century* (New York: Academic Press, 1974).
3. Ewen and Ewen, *Typecasting: On the Arts and Sciences of Human Inequality* (New York: Seven Stories Press, 2006), 11.
4. Wallerstein, *The Modern World-System.*
5. Ewen and Ewen, *Typecasting*, 13.
6. Ewen and Ewen, *Typecasting*, 13.

7. Ewen and Ewen, *Typecasting*, 15.
8. Ewen and Ewen, *Typecasting*, 16.
9. Ewen and Ewen, *Typecasting*, 16.
10. Ignatiev, *How the Irish Became White*, 35.
11. Ignatiev, *How the Irish Became White*, 34–35.
12. Ignatiev, *How the Irish Became White*, 2.
13. Ignatiev, *How the Irish Became White*, 2.
14. Ignatiev, *How the Irish Became White*, 34.
15. Ignatiev, *How the Irish Became White*, 34.
16. Ignatiev, *How the Irish Became White*, 35.
17. For further exploration, also see David R. Roediger's brilliant work, *The Wages of Whiteness: Race and the Making of the American Working Class*, rev. ed. (London: Verso, 1991).
18. Terry Golway, *The Irish in America*, ed. Michael Coffey (New York: Hyperion, 1997), 4.
19. Golway, *The Irish in America*, 5.
20. Golway, *The Irish in America*, 5.
21. F. W. Hirst, *From Adam Smith to Philip Snowden: A history of free trade in Great Britain* (London: T. Fisher Unwin, 1925).
22. Charles Trevelyan in Golway, *The Irish in America*, 14.
23. Golway, *The Irish in America*, 14.
24. Golway, *The Irish in America*, 5.
25. Golway, *The Irish in America*, 3.
26. Golway, *The Irish in America*, 3.
27. Golway, *The Irish in America*, 5.
28. Golway, *The Irish in America*, 22–23.
29. A. C. Crowther, *The Workhouse System 1834–1929: The History of an English Social Institution* (Batsford Academic and Educational, 1981).
30. Golway, *The Irish in America*, 19.
31. Golway, *The Irish in America*, 14–15.
32. Golway, *The Irish in America*, 15.
33. Frank McCourt in Golway, *The Irish in America*, 8.
34. Ignatiev, *How the Irish Became White*, 38.
35. Ignatiev, *How the Irish Became White*, 39.
36. Ignatiev, *How the Irish Became White*, 38.
37. Ignatiev, *How the Irish Became White*, 38.
38. Golway, *The Irish in America*, 7.
39. Personal family documents, 1995.
40. Carl Wittke in Ignatiev, *How the Irish Became White*, 39.
41. Ignatiev, *How the Irish Became White*, 7.
42. Daniel O'Connell in Ignatiev, *How the Irish Became White*, 7.
43. Ignatiev, *How the Irish Became White*, 41.
44. Quoted in Ignatiev, *How the Irish Became White*, 40–41.
45. Ignatiev, *How the Irish Became White*, 41.
46. Ignatiev, *How the Irish Became White*, 38.

47. Roediger, *The Wages of Whiteness.*
48. Ignatiev, *How the Irish Became White*, 95.
49. Ignatiev, *How the Irish Became White*, 95.
50. Roediger, *The Wages of Whiteness.*
51. W. E. B. Du Bois, *Black Reconstruction in the United States* (New York: Harcourt, Brace and Company, 1935).
52. Roediger, *The Wages of Whiteness*, 6.
53. Roediger, *The Wages of Whiteness*, 13.
54. Roediger, *The Wages of Whiteness*, 12.
55. Roediger, *The Wages of Whiteness*, 6.
56. For an insightful critique of Roediger's *Wages of Whiteness*, please do see Theodore W. Allen, "On Roediger's *Wages of Whiteness*," *Cultural Logic* 4, no. 2 (Spring 2001).

4 The Production of Animal Life: The Early American Cattle Business

1. Eric B. Ross, "Patterns of Diet and Forces of Production: An Economic and Ecological History of the Ascendancy of Beef in the United States Diet," in *Beyond the Myths of Culture: Essays in Cultural Materialism*, ed. Eric B. Ross (New York: Academic Press, 1980), 190.
2. Ross, "Patterns of Diet and Forces of Production," 190.
3. Ross, "Patterns of Diet and Forces of Production," 190.
4. Ross, "Patterns of Diet and Forces of Production," 191.
5. Ross, "Patterns of Diet and Forces of Production," 191.
6. Ross, "Patterns of Diet and Forces of Production," 192.
7. Jimmy M. Skaggs, *Prime Cut: Livestock Raising and Meatpacking in the United States, 1607–1983* (College Station: Texas A and M University Press, 1986), 13.
8. Skaggs, *Prime Cut*, 13.
9. Skaggs, *Prime Cut*, 13.
10. Skaggs, *Prime Cut*, 13–14.
11. Ross, "Patterns of Diet and Forces of Production," 186.
12. Skaggs, *Prime Cut*, 15.
13. Skaggs, *Prime Cut*, 16.
14. Skaggs, *Prime Cut*, 17–18.
15. Skaggs, *Prime Cut*, 18.
16. Skaggs, *Prime Cut*, 18.
17. Paul C. Henlein, *Cattle Kingdom in the Ohio Valley, 1783–1860* (Lexington: University of Kentucky Press, 1959), 4.
18. Michael Pollan, *The Omnivore's Dilemma: A Natural History of Four Meals* (New York: The Penguin Press, 2006), 18.
19. Pollan, *The Omnivore's Dilemma*, 18.
20. Pollan, *The Omnivore's Dilemma*, 19.
21. Pollan, *The Omnivore's Dilemma*, 19.

22. Pollan, *The Omnivore's Dilemma*, 25.
23. Pollan, *The Omnivore's Dilemma*, 19.
24. Pollan, *The Omnivore's Dilemma*, 23.
25. Pollan, *The Omnivore's Dilemma*, 25–26.
26. Pollan, *The Omnivore's Dilemma*, 27.
27. Pollan, *The Omnivore's Dilemma*, 27–28.
28. Pollan, *The Omnivore's Dilemma*, 41.
29. E. P. Thompson, "Time, Work-Discipline, and Industrial Capitalism," *Past and Present* II (1967): 58.
30. Thompson, "Time, Work-Discipline, and Industrial Capitalism," 60.
31. Thompson, "Time, Work-Discipline, and Industrial Capitalism," 57.
32. Thompson, "Time, Work-Discipline, and Industrial Capitalism," 57.
33. Thompson, "Time, Work-Discipline, and Industrial Capitalism," 95.
34. Thompson, "Time, Work-Discipline, and Industrial Capitalism," 91.
35. John Foster in Thompson, "Time, Work-Discipline, and Industrial Capitalism," 90.
36. Michel Foucault, *Discipline and Punish: The Birth of the Prison* (New York: Vintage Books, 1979), 154.
37. Thompson, "Time, Work-Discipline, and Industrial Capitalism," 91.
38. Pollan, *The Omnivore's Dilemma*, 193.
39. Ross, "Patterns of Diet and Forces of Production," 204.
40. Henlein, *Cattle Kingdom in the Ohio Valley*, 6.
41. Henlein, *Cattle Kingdom in the Ohio Valley*, 5.
42. Henlein, *Cattle Kingdom in the Ohio Valley*, 5–6.
43. Skaggs, *Prime Cut*, 19.
44. Skaggs, *Prime Cut*, 90.
45. Upton Sinclair, *The Jungle* (New York: Barnes & Noble Classic, 1906/2003).
46. Skaggs, *Prime Cut*, 90.
47. Stuart Ewen, *Captains of Consciousness: Advertising and the Social Roots of the Consumer Culture* (New York: Basic Books, 1976/2001), 23.
48. Skaggs, *Prime Cut*, 108.
49. Ewen, *Captains of Consciousness*, 26–27.
50. Thompson, "Time, Work-Discipline, and Industrial Capitalism."
51. Skaggs, *Prime Cut*, 20.
52. Skaggs, *Prime Cut*, 20.
53. Skaggs, *Prime Cut*, 21.
54. Skaggs, *Prime Cut*, 20.
55. Skaggs, *Prime Cut*, 21.
56. Skaggs, *Prime Cut*, 21.
57. Skaggs, *Prime Cut*, 43.
58. Ross, "Patterns of Diet and Forces of Production," 200.
59. Skaggs, *Prime Cut*, 60.
60. Ross, "Patterns of Diet and Forces of Production," 193.
61. Ross, "Patterns of Diet and Forces of Production," 201.

62. Ross, "Patterns of Diet and Forces of Production," 201–202.
63. Ross, "Patterns of Diet and Forces of Production," 201.
64. Ross, "Patterns of Diet and Forces of Production," 203.
65. Ross, "Patterns of Diet and Forces of Production," 202–203.
66. Ross, "Patterns of Diet and Forces of Production," 203.
67. Reviel Netz, "Collections of Confinement: Thoughts on Barbed Wire," *Connect: Art, Politics, Theory, Practice* 12, no. 1 (2002): 15–22.
68. Skaggs, *Prime Cut*, 61.
69. Skaggs, *Prime Cut*, 61.
70. Skaggs, *Prime Cut*, 63.
71. Skaggs, *Prime Cut*, 64.

5 The Production of Girl Life and the Lives of Girls

1. Cathy Caruth, *Unclaimed Experience: Trauma, Narrative, and History* (Baltimore, MD: The Johns Hopkins University Press, 1996); and Judith Lewis Herman, *Trauma and Recovery: The Aftermath of Violence—From Domestic Abuse to Political Terror* (New York: BasicBooks, 1992).
2. Caruth, *Unclaimed Experience*, 2.
3. For an exploration of radical feminist writing on gendered violence, please do see Susan Brownmiller, *Against Our Will* (New York: Simon and Schuster, 1975); Cassandra Wilson and Noreen Connell, eds., *Rape: The First Sourcebook for Women* (New York: NAL Plume, 1974); Diana E. H. Russell, *The Politics of Rape: The Victim's Perspective* (New York: Stein and Day, 1974); and Diana E. H. Russell, *The Secret Trauma: Incest in the Lives of Girls and Women* (New York: Basic Books, 1986).
4. Jean Halley, *Boundaries of Touch: Parenting and Adult-Child Intimacy* (Urbana, IL: University of Illinois Press, 2007).
5. Halley, *Boundaries of Touch*, 134.
6. Judith Lewis Herman, *Father-Daughter Incest* (Cambridge, MA: Harvard University Press, 1981), 7.
7. Herman, *Father-Daughter Incest*, 4.
8. Timothy Pachirat, *Every Twelve Seconds: Industrialized Slaughter and the Politics of Sight* (New Haven, CT: Yale University Press, 2011); to be discussed further in chapter 7.
9. Jackie Orr, *Panic Diaries: A Genealogy of Panic Disorder* (Durham, NC: Duke University Press, 2006).
10. Nicole Shukin, *Animal Capital: Rendering Life in Biopolitical Times* (Minneapolis: University of Minnesota Press, 2009), 16.
11. Gilles Deleuze, *Essays Critical and Clinical*, trans. D. W. Smith and M. A. Greco (Minneapolis: University of Minnesota Press, 1997), 133.

6 The Lives of Cows

1. Eric B. Ross, "Patterns of Diet and Forces of Production: An Economic and Ecological History of the Ascendancy of Beef in the United States Diet," in *Beyond the Myths of Culture: Essays in Cultural Materialism*, ed. Eric B. Ross (New York: Academic Press, 1980), 204.
2. Michael Pollan, *The Omnivore's Dilemma: A Natural History of Four Meals* (New York: The Penguin Press, 2006), 71.
3. Ross, "Patterns of Diet and Forces of Production," 204.
4. Pollan, *The Omnivore's Dilemma*, 68–69.
5. Eric Schlosser, *Fast Food Nation: The Dark Side of the All-American Meal* (New York: Perennial, 2001), 136.
6. Harold Oppenheimer quoted in Jimmy M. Skaggs, *Prime Cut: Livestock Raising and Meatpacking in the United States, 1607–1983* (College Station: Texas A and M University Press, 1986), 170–171.
7. Michael Pollan, "Power Steer: On the Trail of Industrial Beef," in *The CAFO Reader: The Tragedy of Industrial Animal Factories*, ed. Daniel Imhoff (Berkeley, CA: Watershed Media, 2010), 94.
8. G. M. Ward, P. L. Knox, and B. W. Hobson, "Beef Production Options and Requirements for Fossil Fuel," *Science* 198 (1977): 265.
9. J. J. Harris, H. R. Cross, and J. W. Savell, "History of Meat Grading in the United States," http://meat.tamu.edu/history.html (December 13, 2010).
10. Ward, Knox, and Hobson, "Beef Production Options," 265.
11. Ross, "Patterns of Diet and Forces of Production," 181–225.
12. Pollan, *The Omnivore's Dilemma*, 77.
13. Pollan, *The Omnivore's Dilemma*, 78.
14. Pollan, "Power Steer," 92–108.
15. Pollan, *The Omnivore's Dilemma*, 78.
16. Pollan, *The Omnivore's Dilemma*, 77.
17. Schlosser, *Fast Food Nation*, 142.
18. Daniel Imhoff, "Introduction," in *The CAFO Reader: The Tragedy of Industrial Animal Factories*, ed. Daniel Imhoff (Berkeley, CA: Watershed Media, 2010), xiii.
19. United States Department of Agriculture, "United States Beef and Cattle Industry: Background Statistics and Information," http://www.ers.usda.gov/news/BSECoverage.htm (October 17, 2007).

7 Slaughterhouses and the Death of a Cow

1. Jimmy M. Skaggs, *Prime Cut: Livestock Raising and Meatpacking in the United States, 1607–1983* (College Station: Texas A and M University Press, 1986).
2. Nicole Shukin, *Animal Capital: Rendering Life in Biopolitical Times* (Minneapolis: University of Minnesota Press, 2009).

3. Timothy Pachirat, *Every Twelve Seconds: Industrialized Slaughter and the Politics of Sight* (New Haven, CT: Yale University Press, 2011), Kindle edition.
4. Patricia Nelson Limerick, *The Legacy of Conquest: The Unbroken Past of the American West* (New York: W. W. Norton and Company, 1987).
5. Pachirat, *Every Twelve Seconds.*
6. Pachirat, *Every Twelve Seconds*, Kindle edition, Chapter one.
7. Pachirat, *Every Twelve Seconds*, Kindle edition, Chapter one.
8. For an interesting Foucauldian exploration of race, humans, other animals, and power in slaughterhouses, please do see Stephen Thierman, "Apparatuses of Animality: Foucault Goes to a Slaughterhouse," *Foucault Studies* (September 2010): 89–110.
9. Pachirat, *Every Twelve Seconds*, Kindle edition, notes to Chapter one.
10. Stephen Franklin, "Rights Group Takes Meatpackers to Task," *Chicago Tribune* (26 January 2005), 8.
11. Steven Greenhouse, "US: Meat Packing Industry Criticized on Human Rights Grounds," *New York Times* (January 25, 2005).
12. Skaggs, *Prime Cut.*
13. Karen Olsson, "The Shame of Meatpacking," *The Nation* (September 16, 2002).
14. Gail A. Eisnitz, *Slaughterhouse: The Shocking Story of Greed, Neglect, and Inhumane Treatment Inside of the U.S. Meat Industry* (Amherst, NY: Prometheus Books, 1997), 62.
15. Eisnitz, *Slaughterhouse*, 62.
16. For more information, please do see the Humane Society of the United States, "Factory Farming Campaign: Working to Reduce the Suffering of Animals Raised for Meat, Eggs, and Milk," 2008, http://video.hsus.org/ (July 16, 2008).
17. Humane Society of the United States, "Factory Farming Campaign."
18. Daniel Imhoff, "Introduction," in *The CAFO Reader: The Tragedy of Industrial Animal Factories*, ed. Daniel Imhoff (Berkeley, CA: Watershed Media, 2010), xvi.
19. Imhoff, "Introduction," xv.
20. Eisnitz, *Slaughterhouse*, 20.
21. Eisnitz, *Slaughterhouse*, 20.
22. Imhoff, "Introduction," xvi.
23. Eisnitz, *Slaughterhouse*, 132–133.
24. Upton Sinclair, *The Jungle* (New York: Barnes & Noble Classic, 1906/2003).
25. Maura Spiegel, "Introduction," in Sinclair, *The Jungle*, xv.
26. Sinclair, *The Jungle*, 110.
27. Spiegel, "Introduction," in Sinclair, *The Jungle*, vi.
28. Imhoff, "Introduction," xvi.
29. E. P. Thompson, "Time, Work-Discipline, and Industrial Capitalism," *Past and Present* II (1967): 61.

30. Benjamin Franklin quoted in E. P. Thompson, "Time, Work-Discipline, and Industrial Capitalism," *Past and Present* II (1967): 89.
31. Eisnitz, *Slaughterhouse*, 122.
32. Eisnitz, *Slaughterhouse*, 122.
33. Eisnitz, *Slaughterhouse*, 122.
34. Eisnitz, *Slaughterhouse*, 121.
35. Eisnitz, *Slaughterhouse*, 18.
36. Eisnitz, *Slaughterhouse*, 18–19.
37. Eisnitz, *Slaughterhouse*, 24.
38. Eisnitz, *Slaughterhouse*, 132–133.
39. Eisnitz, *Slaughterhouse*, 166.
40. Eisnitz, *Slaughterhouse*, 188.
41. Eisnitz, *Slaughterhouse*, 189–190.
42. Eisnitz, *Slaughterhouse*, 19.
43. Eisnitz, *Slaughterhouse*, 28.
44. Eisnitz, *Slaughterhouse*, 28.
45. Eisnitz, *Slaughterhouse*, 29.
46. Eisnitz, *Slaughterhouse*, 29.
47. Amy J. Fitzgerald, Linda Kalof, and Thomas Dietz, "Slaughterhouses and Increased Crime Rates: An Empirical Analysis of the Spillover From "The Jungle" Into the Surrounding Community," *Organization Environment* (June 2, 2009).
48. Sinclair, *The Jungle*, 110.
49. Fitzgerald, et al., "Slaughterhouses and Increased Crime Rates," 160.
50. Fitzgerald, et al., "Slaughterhouses and Increased Crime Rates," 164.
51. Fitzgerald, et al., "Slaughterhouses and Increased Crime Rates," 159.
52. Fitzgerald, et al., "Slaughterhouses and Increased Crime Rates," 173.
53. Michael Pollan, "Power Steer: On the Trail of Industrial Beef," in *The CAFO Reader: The Tragedy of Industrial Animal Factories*, ed. Daniel Imhoff (Berkeley, CA: Watershed Media, 2010), 98.
54. Howard F. Lyman, *Mad Cowboy: Plain Truth from the Cattle Rancher Who Won't Eat Meat* (New York: Scribner, 1998), 12.
55. Lyman, *Mad Cowboy.*
56. Frank Burnham quoted in Shukin, *Animal Capital*, 66–67.
57. Shukin, *Animal Capital*, 50.
58. Antonio Negri quoted in Shukin, *Animal Capital*, 78.
59. Shukin, *Animal Capital*, 79.
60. Shukin, *Animal Capital*, 80.
61. Shukin, *Animal Capital*, 67.
62. Pollan, "Power Steer: On the Trail of Industrial Beef," in Imhoff, *The CAFO Reader*, 98.
63. Pollan, "Power Steer: On the Trail of Industrial Beef," in Imhoff, *The CAFO Reader*, 98.

Bibliography

Adams, Scott. *It's Obvious You Won't Survive by Your Wits Alone.* Kansas City, MO: Andrews and McMeel, 1995.

Agamben, Giorgio. *The Open: Man and Animal.* Stanford, CA: Stanford University Press, 2004.

Allen, Theodore W. "On Roediger's *Wages of Whiteness.*" *Cultural Logic* 4, no. 2 (Spring 2001).

Bacon, David. "The Kill-Floor Rebellion." *The American Prospect*, June 30, 2002. http://prospect.org/cs/articles?article=the_killfloor_rebellion.

Bittman, Mark. "Some Animals Are More Equal Than Others." Editorial, *New York Times*, March 15, 2011. http://opinionator.blogs.nytimes.com/2011/03/15/some-animals-are-more-equal-than-others/?emc=eta1.

Brownmiller, Susan. *Against Our Will.* New York: Simon & Schuster, 1975.

Caruth, Cathy. *Unclaimed Experience: Trauma, Narrative, and History.* Baltimore, MD: The Johns Hopkins University Press, 1996.

Clough, Patricia Ticineto, and Jean Halley, eds. *The Affective Turn: Theorizing the Social.* Durham, NC: Duke University Press, 2007.

Crowther, A. C. *The Workhouse System 1834–1929: The History of an English Social Institution.* Athens: The University of Georgia Press, 1981.

Connell, Noreen, and Cassandra Wilson, eds. *Rape: The First Sourcebook for Women.* New York: NAL Plume, 1974.

Deleuze, Gilles. *Essays Critical and Clinical*, translated by D. W. Smith and M. A. Greco. Minneapolis: University of Minnesota Press, 1997.

Du Bois, W. E. B. *Black Reconstruction in the United States.* New York: Harcourt, Brace and Company, 1935.

Eisnitz, Gail A. *Slaughterhouse: The Shocking Story of Greed, Neglect, and Inhumane Treatment Inside the U.S. Meat Industry.* Amherst, NY: Prometheus Books, 1997.

Ewen and Ewen. *Typecasting: On the Arts and Sciences of Human Inequality.* New York: Seven Stories Press, 2006.

Ewen, Stuart. *Captains of Consciousness: Advertising and the Social Roots of the Consumer Culture.* 1976. Reprint, New York: Basic Books, 2001.

Fitzgerald, Amy J., Linda Kalof, and Thomas Dietz. "Slaughterhouses and Increased Crime Rates: An Empirical Analysis of the Spillover From

'The Jungle' Into the Surrounding Community." *Organization & Environment* (June 2009): 158–184.

Foucault, Michel. *The Birth of Biopolitics: Lectures at the College de France, 1978–1979.* New York: Picador, 2008.

———. *Discipline and Punish: The Birth of the Prison.* New York: Vintage Books, 1979.

———. *The History of Sexuality, Volume 1: An Introduction.* Translated by Robert Hurley. New York: Vintage Books, 1978.

———. *Society Must Be Defended: Lectures at the Colleges De France, 1975–1976.* New York: Picador, 2002.

Franklin, Stephen. "Rights Group Takes Meatpackers to Task." *Chicago Tribune*, January 26, 2005.

Greenhouse, Steven. "US: Meat Packing Industry Criticized on Human Rights Grounds." *New York Times*, January 25, 2005.

Golway, Terry. *The Irish in America*, edited by Michael Coffey. New York: Hyperion, 1997.

Halley, Jean. *Boundaries of Touch: Parenting and Adult-Child Intimacy.* Urbana: University of Illinois Press, 2007.

Harris, J. J., H. R. Cross, and J. W. Savell. "History of Meat Grading in the United States." Accessed December 13, 2010. Last modified 1996. http://meat.tamu.edu/history.html.

Henlein, Paul C. *Cattle Kingdom in the Ohio Valley, 1783–1860.* Lexington: University of Kentucky Press, 1959.

Herman, Judith Lewis. *Trauma and Recover: The Aftermath of Violence—From Domestic Abuse to Political Terror.* New York: Basic Books, 1992.

Herman, Judith Lewis. *Father-Daughter Incest.* Cambridge, MA: Harvard University Press, 1981.

Hirst, F. W. *From Adam Smith to Philip Snowden: A History of Free Trade in Great Britain.* London: T. Fisher Unwin, 1925.

Humane Society of the United States. "Factory Farming Campaign: Working to Reduce the Suffering of Animals Raised for Meat, Eggs, and Milk." Accessed July 16, 2008. http://video.hsus.org/.

Ignatiev, Noel. *How the Irish Became White.* New York: Routledge, 1995.

Imhoff, Daniel. Introduction to *The CAFO Reader: The Tragedy of Industrial Animal Factories.* Edited by Daniel Imhoff. Berkeley, CA: Watershed Media, 2010.

———, ed. *The CAFO Reader: The Tragedy of Industrial Animal Factories.* Berkeley, CA: Watershed Media, 2010.

Limerick, Patricia Nelson. *The Legacy of Conquest: The Unbroken Past of the American West.* New York: W. W. Norton and Company, 1987.

Lyman, Howard F. *Mad Cowboy: Plain Truth from the Cattle Rancher Who Won't Eat Meat.* New York: Scribner, 1998.

Netz, Reviel. "Collections of Confinement: Thoughts on Barbed Wire." *Connect: Art, Politics, Theory, Practice* 12, no. 1 (2002): 15–22.

Olsson, Karen. "The Shame of Meatpacking." *The Nation*, September 16, 2002, 11–16.

Orr, Jackie. *Panic Diaries: A Genealogy of Panic Disorder*. Durham, NC: Duke University Press, 2006.

Pachirat, Timothy. *Every Twelve Seconds: Industrialized Slaughter and the Politics of Sight*. New Haven, CT: Yale University Press, 2011.

Pollan, Michael. *The Omnivore's Dilemma: A Natural History of Four Meals*. New York: The Penguin Press, 2006.

———. "Power Steer: On the Trail of Industrial Beef." In *The CAFO Reader: The Tragedy of Industrial Animal Factories*, edited by Daniel Imhoff, 92–108. Berkeley, CA: Watershed Media, 2010.

Public Broadcasting Service (PBS). "New Perspectives on the West: Frederick Jackson Turner, 1861–1932." Accessed on December 3, 2010. http://www.pbs.org/weta/thewest/people/s_z/turner.htm, 2001.

Roediger, David R. *The Wages of Whiteness: Race and the Making of the American Working Class*. Rev. ed. London: Verso, 1991.

Rose, Nikolas. *Powers of Freedom: Reframing Political Thought*. Cambridge: Cambridge University Press, 1999.

———. *The Politics of Life Itself: Biomedicine, Power, and Subjectivity in the Twenty-First Century*. Princeton, NJ: Princeton University Press, 2007.

Ross, Eric B. "Patterns of Diet and Forces of Production: An Economic and Ecological History of the Ascendancy of Beef in the United States Diet." In *Beyond the Myths of Culture: Essays in Cultural Materialism*, edited by Eric B. Ross, 181–225. New York: Academic Press, 1980.

Russell, Diana E. H. *The Politics of Rape: The Victim's Perspective*. New York: Stein and Day, 1974.

———. *The Secret Trauma: Incest in the Lives of Girls and Women*. New York: Basic Books, 1986.

Schlosser, Eric. *Fast Food Nation: The Dark Side of the All-American Meal*. New York: Perennial, 2001.

———. "Hog Hell: Smithfield's Workers Face a Modern-Day Jungle." *The Nation*, September 11, 2006.

Segal, Jacob. "Freedom and Normalization: Poststructuralism and the Liberalism of Michael Oakeshott." *American Political Science Review* 97, no. 3 (August 2003): 447.

Shukin, Nicole. *Animal Capital: Rendering Life in Biopolitical Times*. Minneapolis: University of Minnesota Press, 2009.

Sinclair, Upton. *The Jungle*. 1906. Reprint, New York: Barnes & Noble Classic, 2003.

Skaggs, Jimmy M. *Prime Cut: Livestock Raising and Meatpacking in the United States, 1607–1983*. College Station: Texas A and M University Press, 1986.

Slotkin, Richard. *Gunfighter Nation: The Myth of the Frontier in the Twentieth Century America*. New York: HarperCollins Publishers, Inc., 1992.

Spiegel, Maura. Introduction to *The Jungle*. Upton Sinclair. Reprint, New York: Barnes & Noble Classic, 2003.

Thierman, Stephen. "Apparatuses of Animality: Foucault Goes to a Slaughterhouse." *Foucault Studies* (September 2010): 89–110.

Thompson, E. P. "Time, Work-Discipline, and Industrial Capitalism." *Past and Present* (1967): 56–97.

Tomaselli, Paige, and Meredith Niles. "Changing the Law: The Road to Reform." In *The CAFO Reader: The Tragedy of Industrial Animal Factories*, edited by Daniel Imhoff, 314–329. Berkeley, CA: Watershed Media, 2010.

Turner, Frederick Jackson. *The Frontier in American History*. Tucson: The University of Arizona Press, 1920/1994.

United States Department of Agriculture. "United States Beef and Cattle Industry: Background Statistics and Information." Last modified October 17, 2007. http://www.ers.usda.gov/news/BSECoverage.htm.

Wallerstein, Immanuel Maurice. *The Modern World-System: Capitalist Agriculture and the Origins of the European World-Economy in the Sixteenth Century*. New York: Academic Press, 1974.

Ward, G. M., P. L. Knox, and B. W. Hobson. "Beef Productions Options and Requirements for Fossil Fuel." *Science* 198 (1977): 265–271.

Wilson, Cassandra, and Noreen Connell, eds. *Rape: The First Sourcebook for Women*. New York: NAL Plume, 1974.

Biographical Statement

Jean Halley is an associate professor of sociology at the College of Staten Island of the City University of New York (CUNY). She earned her doctorate in sociology at the Graduate Center at CUNY, and her master's degree in theology at Harvard University. Her book about touching children, breastfeeding, children's sleep, and contemporary childrearing advice, *Boundaries of Touch: Parenting and Adult-Child Intimacy,* was published in July 2007 by the University of Illinois Press. She also assisted Patricia Ticineto Clough in editing *The Affective Turn: Theorizing the Social* (Duke University Press, 2007). More recently, she coauthored *Seeing White: An Introduction to White Privilege and Race* (Rowman & Littlefield, 2011) with Amy Eshleman and Ramya Vijaya.

Index

CPSIA information can be obtained
at www.ICGtesting.com
Printed in the USA
LVHW081131130721
692566LV00011B/929

9 781349 296514